ONLY OLD ONCE !

by

Valerie McLean

Introducing creativity into elderly care

Published by
© Valerie McLean

Cover designs by Andrea McLean
Other illustrations by Valerie McLean

Typesetting by Stuart McLean

Printed by Hobbs the Printers, Southampton

All rights reserved. Apart from pages marked for photocopying no part of this publication may be reproduced, stored in a retrieval system, or transmitted in any form or by any means electronic or mechanical, including photocopying without permission in writing from the publisher.

A CIP catalogue record for this book is available from the British Library.

ISBN 0 9530329 0 6

Acknowledgements

I would like to thank:

All the elderly people in Gloucestershire and Herefordshire with whom I have worked and from whom I have learnt so much.
My sons and daughter, who have helped me with the production of this book.
My colleagues and friends (especially Mary Martin) from Artspace Cinderford, and the Royal Forest of Dean College for their support and exchange of ideas.
Don Bradley, Head of Faculty for Continuing Education at the Royal Forest of Dean College for his support for educational projects for older people.
To Joan North for permission to print, Geriatric Ward from her book of poems entitled Poems, Sense and Nonsense ISBN 0-9527429-0-X.

ONLY OLD ONCE !

Introducing creativity into elderly care

by Valerie McLean

"For age is opportunity no less
than youth itself in another dress,
And as the evening twilight fades away
the sky is filled with stars invisible by day."
Poem by Longfellow.

About The Author

Valerie McLean is a trained nurse, experienced in the care of the elderly. She also teaches arts and crafts and has worked for the past eight years on projects with elderly people in Gloucestershire initiated by; Artshape Gloucestershire, Artspace Cinderford, and The Royal Forest of Dean College.

Introducing This Book

The information in this book can be used by anyone involved with improving the quality of life for elderly people, referred to as, 'clients' in most instances for continuity.
The title 'clients' is to include: patients, residents, students, or members, living in or attending; nursing homes, sheltered accommodation, residential homes, hospitals, day centres, and clubs, referred to as nursing homes and centres.

The language, format and subject matter have been chosen with the intention of producing a 'user friendly' handbook containing well tested ideas for activities.

As we become older we have progressively more leisure time, but unfortunately, sometimes we have to rely more and more on others to help provide leisure activities. Without that help we may do less and less.

In British society, negative expectations of ageing are the norm, but all who work with elderly people are well placed to improve this impression. Elderly people need control over their lives, and need to be able to fill their days in an enjoyable, active and challenging way. We need to open up possibilities and avoid the attitude that Florence Nightingale developed in latter life.
At the age of 65 years, she wrote in her diary; "Today oh Lord, let me dedicate this crumbling old woman to thee." And then went on to live another 25 years as a self-imposed invalid.

I hope that the ideas in this book will help elderly people to live life to the full.

Valerie McLean 1997

CONTENTS

CHAPTER ONE OPPORTUNITIES AND CONSIDERATIONS	7
IMPROVING THE QUALITY OF NURSING HOME RESIDENTS' LEISURE TIME	7
FRIENDSHIP	9
CATERING FOR THE LONER	9
HEALTH CONSIDERATIONS	10
SETTING UP AND RUNNING A REGULAR GROUP ACTIVITY	15
CHAPTER TWO MENTAL EXERCISE	19
RATIONALE	19
MEMORY GAMES	20
DISCUSSION GROUPS	23
REMINISCENCE	25
A BOOK OF MEMORIES	28
CHAPTER THREE SONG AND VERSE	37
RATIONALE	37
SINGING	38
TRADITIONAL SONGS	40
POETRY	42
CHAPTER FOUR ARTS AND CRAFTS	45
RATIONALE	45
SIMPLE JEWELLERY MAKING - BEADS	46
POTTERY	48
WATER COLOUR PAINTING	50
POINTS TO REMEMBER FOR PAINTING SESSIONS	51
THERAPEUTIC PAINTING SESSIONS	52
DOUGH CRAFT	53
DECORATING PAPER - MARBLING	54
DECORATING PAPER - MONOPRINTING	55
MORE PRINTMAKING - LEAF PRINTS	56
BLOCKPRINTING	57
DECORATING PAPER - STENCILLING	58
ANOTHER GREETING CARD IDEA	62
PAPIER-MÂCHÉ	63
DECOUPAGE	64
3-D MODERN DECOUPAGE	65
PRESERVING FLOWERS	66
PRESSED FLOWERS	67
PROJECT - DECORATE A SMALL BOX	67

Flower Arranging	68
Potpourri	69
Paper Flowers	70
Knitting	71
Rugs	72
Patchwork	74
Cross Stitch	76
Crochet	77
Health and Safety Hints for Craft Sessions	78
Home Crafts	79

CHAPTER FIVE OUTINGS, EVENTS AND ENTERTAINMENT — 81

Rationale	81
Outings	82
Events and Entertainment	83

CHAPTER SIX SEASONAL ACTIVITIES AND THEME DAYS — 85

Rationale	85
Christmas Projects	86
Easter Projects	91
Egg Decorating	92
Harvest Festival	93
Remembrance Sunday	94

CHAPTER SEVEN EXERCISE AND RELAXATION — 95

Rationale	95
Armchair Exercises	96
Relaxation	98

CHAPTER EIGHT MISCELLANEOUS — 100

New Beginnings and Achievements for over Sixties	100
Client Social Care Sheet	102
Activities Timetable	104
A Newsletter for the Home or Centre	108
Useful Contacts	109
Bibliography	110

Chapter One Opportunities and Considerations

Improving the Quality of Nursing Home Residents' Leisure Time

- Find time to talk one to one with clients and their relatives to hear about previous skills and hobbies, and record in the Care Plan.

- Develop a positive attitude from staff in attaching importance to group and individual activities.

- Find access to sufficient space for recreation, to include a quiet room and outdoor seating if possible.

- Encourage clients to organise activities for themselves whenever possible.

- Encourage very confused clients to help with familiar jobs such as folding washing etc. in a non patronising way.

- Be watchful for ways to vary the daily routine. Sometimes something as simple as a care assistant wheeling someone in their wheelchair a long way round, through part of the garden to the Dining Room, will make a difference to that clients day.

- Have a variety of nostalgic music tapes to play regularly.

- Keep an eye on the television to make sure that someone is actually watching it.

- Is there a piano or organ?
  Can any member of staff or client be encouraged to play?

- Invite the 'outside world in' whenever possible.
  For example, Could the local W.I. hold the occasional meeting in the Dining Room?

- Offer opportunities for further education. For example, would the local college be prepared to consider the 'craft room' as a venue for an evening class?

- Consider the communal living areas.
  Are the chairs arranged in small groups around a coffee table, so that people can talk naturally?
  Are there books, including Large Print, easily available?
  Are there pictures, clocks, and mirrors on the walls?

- Consider ways to add interest, for example, could a bird table be placed outside a Living Room window?

- Are there living plants inside?

- Encourage visits from (docile!) pets. Is there a house pet?
  A blind lady regularly visited one home that I worked in, always bringing her golden retriever to everyone for a pat. Everyone thoroughly enjoyed this event especially the dog.

- Provide double rooms for married couples or partners and except as natural behaviour that people can fall in love at any age.

- Arrange a regular visit from the hairdresser.

- Give clients the opportunity to choose and buy their own clothes from mail order or visiting dealers.

- Would someone benefit from a manicure? This gives an opportunity for one to one conversation. Be sure to consider the whole person. If the client is confused, and unable to make considered choices, you will have to make those choices for her. A farmers wife who has never worn make-up, may enjoy having a manicure and then her hands massaged with hand cream But bright red nail polish would be inappropriate.
  A container could be obtained to hold creams, cotton wool, emery boards etc.
  The Red Cross organisation provide volunteers to give manicures.

- Consider offering sensory stimulation, such as burning fragrance oils on an oil burner to provide different smells.

- Give consideration to clients from ethnic minorities, in order to respect differing customs and religious beliefs.

- Organise group meetings
  For the elderly person, living in a nursing home, sheltered accommodation, or living with relatives and attending a day centre, regular group meetings may provide a landmark during the week. It is an opportunity for ideas to be exchanged, and for friendships to be made in the relaxed atmosphere. Often, for the Elderly Mentally Infirm, problems areas such as orientation and reasoning are helped.
  Nurses/carers/teachers organising leisure activities, for groups and individuals, can benefit from the stimulation and learning experience, and perhaps even view the elderly in a new light. If we manage to have fun and raise lots of laughter amongst our group we give something more valuable than a dose of medicine.

Friendship

I feel that a major consideration when encouraging most clients into leisure activities, is that friendship can then flourish more easily, which is so important for the mental well-being of most people. I can recall an extremely confused old lady entering a nursing home where I worked, who was lonely despite a supportive family and had an imaginary friend. After a few months another very confused, rather disagreeable (it has to be said) old lady came to live in the home, and the two became inseparable, always sitting together, chatting and laughing.

The conversations did not always seem to make sense to staff in passing, but the pleasure found in each others company was obvious. Both the ladies then appeared more caring to everyone else.

*"How sweet, how passing sweet, is solitude!
But grant me still a friend in my retreat,
Whom I may whisper--solitude is sweet."*
Cowper, from 'Retirement',1782

Catering For the Loner

Depending on their capabilities, clients who do not wish to be part of a group, can still be encouraged to widen their horizons.

The 'Loner' could be kept in touch with the programme of events, so that he or she would feel welcome at any time.

Ideas for individual projects

- An individual craft project e.g. knitting baby clothes, making craft items for a summer fête.

- Individual games e.g. patience

- Gardening e.g. taking cuttings from house plants, growing a tomato plant in the conservatory.

- An Elderly Mentally Infirm client may enjoy making a Memory Diary containing photographs, writings and memorabilia.

- Anything is possible for someone who is mentally able, for example, learning a language or writing a novel.
  A word processor is much easier to use than a type writer, especially for a disabled person.

We must have regard for everyone's right to privacy and to be left alone for some of the time.

Health Considerations

Often the activities organiser is not a trained nurse. It is worth he or she being aware of the more frequently occurring health problems of the elderly and how leisure activities can be beneficial.

Cardiovascular Diseases

Cardiovascular diseases are a major problem in the western world, as they account for the largest proportion of deaths and a great deal of disability, including: breathlessness, pain , fluid retention, insomnia and confusion.
Angina pectoris is chest pain due to lack of nourishment of the heart muscle.
Arteriosclerosis is the build up of fatty deposits in the blood vessels, which can result in, blood clots(thrombosis), heart diseases and stroke.
Heart failure occurs when the heart cannot cope with pumping blood all around the body, and may be a result of hypertension (high blood pressure).
Doctors and nurses treat clients with cardiovascular diseases with drugs, diet, nursing care and advice on lifestyle. As a stressful lifestyle is thought to be a contributory factor, we should try to relieve anxiety by keeping the environment as calm as possible and offer the opportunity to learn relaxation skills.

Decline in muscle power and sense of balance

It is vitally important to encourage regular exercise to slow down the inevitable decline in muscle power. The decline in position sense can result in elderly people becoming less steady on their feet. This can be allowed for by the provision of rails, furniture, and good lighting

Diabetes Mellitus

In this disease, the body does not adequately regulate glucose levels in the blood, resulting in thirst, weight loss, frequent passing of urine. Diabetes is treated with appropriate diet and medication. Nursing staff can advise should any activity involve food or drink.

Lung Disease

Chronic Bronchitis and Emphysema are conditions where damage has occurred to the airways, resulting in breathlessness and the ineffective transfer of oxygen from air to blood. The most important environmental consideration is cigarette smoking, which should not be allowed during leisure activities where non-smokers are present.

Osteoarthritis

Worn joints produce painful movements, which results in less and less mobility for the sufferer, who should be encouraged to move around as much as possible. Doctors and physiotherapists treat this condition, and if the damage is severe, surgery can be recommended.

Pressure Sores

Few of us are at risk from pressure sores, because we move when we are uncomfortable. Disabled elderly people cannot always move freely, so the blood supply to a section of skin is cut off, resulting in tissue breakdown if pressure is not relieved. Nurses and care staff work hard to prevent pressure sores developing. Any activity increasing the number of changes of position is very valuable, plus the provision of adequate cushioning to support and make our clients as comfortable as possible.

Communication Problems

Parkinson's disease and stroke are examples of diseases affecting older people where the victims are likely to have difficulty in communicating.

Points to Remember when Speaking with Clients who have Communication Problems

- Make eye contact.
- Use language appropriate to age, using normal tone.
- Allow time, and listen carefully to answers and be aware of body language.
- Stop others answering for the client.
- Remove background noise if possible.

Parkinson's disease

This common disorder affects the part of the brain involved with movement, so that the sufferer often has a shuffling gait, a tremor, and slowness of movement.
The lack of facial expression can give the illusion that he or she is unaware, so we should give time for the client to respond when spoken to. Beneath the apparent lethargic exterior there is often a frustrated, intelligent individual and we should try not to increase the feelings of isolation by underestimating ability. Getting out of a chair can be difficult, as starting a movement is often a problem. Doctors and physiotherapists treat this extremely distressing disease, and we should do all that we can to encourage the client to benefit from leisure activities.

Stroke

A stroke is caused by an interruption of the blood supply to the brain, caused by a haemorrhage or blockage. This can lead to paralysis down one side, speech difficulties, confusion, limited concentration, urinary incontinence etc.
Considerable teamwork involving doctors, nurses, occupational therapists, speech therapists helps achieve as high a level of independence as possible for the client. Anything that we can do to encourage the stroke victim to be involved in leisure activities, will be helpful.
A relaxed attitude helps when relating to a frustrated client with speech problems, who may not be aware that his or her words are not formed correctly. Phrase questions so that the client can answer yes or no if the speech difficulties are severe.
During craft sessions, perhaps a carer could sit nearby to offer a helping hand, allowing him or her to take an active part.
Chairs must give enough support and height, extra pillows can be provided and there must be adequate room for wheelchairs around the table.

Deafness

Special considerations for clients with hearing difficulties include:

- Try to face the client when addressing.
- With more dependent clients, discreetly make sure that hearing aids are turned on and properly adjusted to avoid the problem of high pitched whistles.
- When speaking to an elderly deaf person, one can be asked to "speak up". As soon as one speaks louder, one is met with the retort, "There is no need to shout, I am not deaf!" It seems that a characteristic problem of deafness associated with ageing, is that vowels are easier to hear than consonants, so try to accentuate the consonants.
- Elderly deaf people are able to follow conversation easier at a slower rate, where there is no background noise.

Sight Impairment

In Cataract, the lens of the eye becomes opaque and an operation may be necessary. Glaucoma occurs when there is increased pressure inside the eye due to a build up of fluid.

Special considerations for clients with sight defects include:

- The provision of large print and Braille for bingo cards, books, song sheets
- Retaining the usual position of furniture whenever possible
- Providing the support of a care worker sitting nearby.
- Considering the programme content.

Ideas for groups with sensory problems

- Making pot pourri,
- Guessing the smell - Fill small containers with foodstuffs.
- Guess the object in the bag.
- Discussion groups.
- A musical quiz.
- Tactile crafts such as modelling clay, salt dough etc.
- Naming different coins by touch.

Depression

A common problem for elderly people is depression, the symptoms of which include loss of appetite, sleeplessness and feelings of despair. Anxiety can be helped by learning relaxation techniques, or having someone to talk to in natural counselling situations, such as having a hairdo or a manicure. Some physical illnesses such as Parkinson's disease are associated with depression, and some medicines have depression as a side effect. Bereavement is as hard to cope with at eighty as it is at twenty, and sometimes people have had to lose their home as well as friends and relatives. Elderly people whose close friends may have died, and whose family live a long way away, may lack someone to confide in. The kindest thing to do for a bereaved person is to be there and listen when needed.

A discussion group theme may enable clients to talk about their feelings, which can do much to alleviate fears and reinforce positive thoughts. Leisure activities can help to raise mood, once we have managed to coax the client to join the group, or have a go with something on their own, if preferred. Whilst living in a residential home it is possible for the clients to have too little stress in their lives. So we have to create a healthy balance to provide sufficient stimulation.

Dementia

Several organic disease processes causes dementia of which Alzheimer's Disease is the most well known. Usually the symptoms of memory loss, personality changes and loss of intellectual abilities, develop gradually and there is no cure.

It is not easy to assess the abilities of dementing clients, and while we must not talk down or treat any client as a child, we also do not want to offer an activity that is going to frustrate or lower self esteem. Somehow everyone's needs have to be assessed individually.

Working with dementing elderly clients in nursing homes is undervalued and can be physically and mentally exhausting. But the work can bring enormous job satisfaction especially if the quality of life is raised for the client, by offering a varied and relaxed routine to the day.

Activity sessions will probably be quite short and well prepared, with a high staff to client ratio.

Ideas for activity sessions for dementing clients

- Therapeutic Painting Sessions are sometimes successful.
- Craft sessions are sometimes successful as long as there are enough members of staff available to help, and the emphasis is on the process rather than the end product.
- Reminiscence, looking at old photographs, books etc.
- Armchair exercises.
- Sing-a-longs.

Remember that it is the engaging of the clients attention and improving the feelings of self worth that is important, rather than an end product.

More Considerations for Clients suffering from Dementia

A Reality Orientation Board with Day, Place, Season, Date, Weather etc. will help with memory loss, as will the provision of clear labels on doors of toilets and bedrooms.

I am not of the view that clients who are firmly back in the past should be constantly brought into the here and now. After all we all create our own reality around us.

Our expectations of what can be achieved by the client group must be laid down with considerations of the clients day to day behaviour pattern. For example, consider a lady who spends each day in an anxious state, trying to find her long deceased mother. For this client to sit calmly for ten minutes looking through old photographs would be a very positive achievement.

The clients bedroom, or corner of a bedroom can be made to reflect his or her personality as much as possible, and not appear the same as everyone else's. For example, has the client photographs and items from the past on display? If the client has always been keen on make up and jewellery, is there a make up mirror and jewellery box? If the client has always been a keen gardener has he or she been encouraged to put up a gardening calendar, or pick a few flowers from the garden?

These considerations can help the client suffering from dementia to distinguish his or her own bedroom and feel at home.

Multi-Sensory Environments

Multi--Sensory Environments are a recent addition to the options open to professionals working in the field of elderly care. Known as Snoezelen (an amalgam of the Dutch words for sniff and doze), this treatment or activity was developed in the 1980s in Holland as a way of providing a relaxing and stimulating environment for people with severe learning difficulties. A room can be set aside and fitted out with lighting equipment, an image projector, suitable furniture, burners for essential oils and a sound system for relaxation tapes.

There is some evidence[1] that Snoezelen may improve the quality of life for older people suffering from dementia and we can look forward to further evidence of these improvements in the future. Beside providing relaxation, there appears be an increase in mental and physical activity for clients introduced into the Snoezelen room. T.F.H. supply advice and equipment.(Refer to contacts page)

---

[1] Savage P. Snoezelen for Confused older people: some concerns
'Elderly Care' Dec/Jan 1997

Setting up and Running a Regular Group Activity

After enlisting the support of staff and talking to clients, decisions regarding time, place and programme content need to be made.

Time

Most nursing home staff prefer sessions in the afternoon, when a lull in the routine work occurs. From my observation, it does seem to be the case that confused and anxious clients have a more settled day if an activity session during the morning has given a sense of achievement. After lunch the siesta usually lasts until after 2.30pm when everyone is anticipating a cup of tea. So, around 3pm is a good time for an afternoon activity session.
In clubs and day centres, morning and afternoon sessions work equally well.

Place

A neutral space is usually recommended, away from communal living areas in order to give more choice, although in some hospitals/nursing homes a neutral space is hard to find. This facility is sometimes very important for certain groupwork, for example, for therapeutic painting sessions.
There are advantages to holding some activities in the lounge area, at least for the first few sessions, as the less confident client will often be happier to stay in a familiar chair and watch a regular craft activity for several weeks before eventually joining in.

Content

The first session will hopefully be an opportunity for everyone to voice their opinion on programme content, followed by something to get everyone chatting - i.e. a browse through some old photographs and a discussion about how life has changed. The programme will develop as the weeks go on, as for example, clay work may become very popular or poetry reading very successful. The group members may decide to invite a specialist along, for example a physiotherapist, to advise on armchair exercises, or the local spinners guild to demonstrate skills. The possibilities are endless.

Suggestions to Group Leaders

Be Prepared

- Publicise well with posters and informal discussion between staff and clients.
- Try not to clash with other events(e.g. Coronation Street on T.V.!) .
- Prepare room and set up materials beforehand. e.g. Chairs in a semi-circle without a table for discussion groups. I was once told by a client that she objected to the chairs being in a semi-circle rather than against the walls because people argued more! The general opinion of the group was that the stimulation of a heated discussion was a positive experience.
- Check discreetly if clients need their hearing aids or spectacles.
- Be punctual and welcome new members.
- Use the names that clients prefer to be called by.

Be Aware of Body Language

- Make eye contact.
- Smile and look interested.
- Touch can be very reassuring to elderly people.

During Discussion Groups

- Encourage clients to talk to one another and not to direct their opinions to the Group Leader all the time.
- Discourage staff from talking to one another.
- Ask open ended questions (e.g. "What was it like trying to organise a wedding in wartime?" rather than - "Did you get married during the War?").
- Remember elderly people often take a long time to explain things.
- Retain confidentiality.

Be Open To New Ideas

- Never say 'I am not artistic'
- Ask for the clients opinion on the session at the end.
- All staff attending the session should join in with the activity, even if it is a Sing-Song!

Most Important - *Raise a Laugh!*

Any activity group whether craft, discussion, bingo, or whatever, the stimulation appears to bring about social interchange. Just the coming together into a group or sitting in a different room results in a great deal of extra conversation.

Problems To Overcome

Lack of Motivation

By far the most common problem, is reluctance from the clients, especially when they have been used to sitting for long periods of time in a non communicative fashion. All we can do is to try our best and accept that we will fail to motivate some clients to benefit from any activities. It is, after all, their choice.
It often happens that a group member will say that they are pleased that they were persuaded to join the group, so we have to know how far to go in trying to attract a client.

Disruptive Behaviour

During discussion sessions, a very dominant member may have been encouraged at the start, as there was anxiety that no-one would contribute. Now he or she can be discouraged from dominating the proceedings by skillfully bringing in someone else at a suitable moment, or arranging chairs so that the dominant members are not always sitting opposite the group leader.
Occasionally, one encounters an uninhibited client, who takes the opportunity to hold centre stage. He or she may be making lewd remarks or singing bawdy songs, or as has happened in one of my groups an extrovert lady enjoying pulling outrageous faces during discussion groups! The group will more than likely howl with laughter. We certainly do not wish to become too serious but eventually we may have to distract the offending member, and try to channel his or her energy elsewhere.

Reluctant Group Members

If someone wishes to leave the group for no apparent reason, after a gentle persuasion to stay, let him or her go, but invite him or her back next time.
Hopefully a naturally shy person will usually gradually gain confidence as the weeks go by. A depressed member who may be incommunicative and withdrawn, may need the support of a trusted member of staff at first, sitting nearby.

A Group Member Becomes Anxious

If someone should become very upset he or she can be invited to share feelings with a well established group. I am always touched at how kind and supportive elderly people are towards one another in this situation.

The Numbers Of Members Dramatically Drops.

Some days it is more difficult than others to gather the group members together. Do not give up. The next week may be completely different. Is the session planned at a suitable time? Is the programme interesting enough? Are the staff sufficiently motivated?

The Activities Programme - Content

We can divide the range of activities into the following groups:

- Mental Exercise - Orientation, Memory games and Quizzes.
- Discussion and Reminiscence.
- Song and Verse.
- Arts and Crafts.
- Home Crafts.
- Events, Outings and Entertainment.
- Seasonal Activities and Theme Days.
- Exercise and Relaxation.

Client Consultation

We should be doing all that we can to consult with clients whilst setting up the programme. The initial recording in the care plan when clients first join the centre or nursing home is of prime importance, as this is when expectations are laid down.

More Ways of Consulting Clients:
◊ Suggestion Box
◊ Residents Committee
◊ Informal Discussion between staff and client(s)

I have found the informal discussion to be the most productive, when trying to set up the first sessions.

Funding

Although no one should be excluded on poverty grounds, I feel that is dignified for the elderly clients to pay towards their entertainment, craft materials etc., if they would normally do so outside the home or centre.
Some craft activities are self funding once set up, as extra items can be made and put on sale, but the clients can still be invited to contribute.

Chapter Two Mental Exercise

Rationale

Mental stimulation is an ongoing necessity to maintain mental capabilities. Quizzes will encourage conversation and often raise a laugh.

Cognitive skills are practised such as carrying out instructions and writing. The stimulation of both recent and long term memory improves concentration.

Clients who have physical disabilities and find activities involving mobility and dexterity difficult can often shine during a quiz.

English Grammar was an important subject on the school timetable for many elderly people, so mentally buried information often surfaces during word games involving synonyms, similes, homonyms etc. giving a feeling of self-worth.

Memory and brainstorming games, possibly using a flip chart, can be used in all group situations whatever the ability.

Clients are encouraged to speak out in the group situation, allowing confidence to grow.

Chapter Two Mental Exercise

Memory Games

Table Games

Table Games include Scrabble™, dominoes, and drafts.
Elderly mentally infirm clients often do well at games such as Scrabble, with some support.
A Board game, such as Ludo, can be much easier for a group of elderly clients to play if a large board is made.
Copy the layout onto a large square of strong cardboard (One metre square, for example). The different coloured sections can be filled in with paint or felt tip pen. A large dice can be bought from an educational supplier. A very large Scrabble board is available from T.F.H. (refer to contacts page)

Flipchart Games

Word Games -
Whilst a flip chart is not essential, it is a help. Sometimes it is appropriate to ask individual clients to answer, sometimes the group as a whole, and sometimes two or more teams.

Suggestions for word games

Write a long word in large letters and ask the group to make as many words as possible from it.

Homonyms (pairs of words that sound the same but are different in meaning and spelling)
Everyone to think of as many as possible. Divide into teams if appropriate.
e.g. pairs and pears
   serial and cereal
   foul and fowl

Create a word square with help from everyone in the group.

Write up the first half of a proverb or famous quote, and ask the group to finish it off.
e.g

He who hesitates __	A new broom __
Absence makes __	A miss is as __
Hope springs eternal __	All that glitters __
If at first you don't __	A friend in need __
To err is human __	Proof of the pudding __
An eye for an eye __	You cannot get blood __
A trouble shared __	Birds of a feather __
He who pays the piper __	A stitch in time __

Encourage the group to discuss whether or not they agree with the sentiment expressed.

How many animals (or flowers, birds etc.) can you think of beginning with each letter of the alphabet?

Guess The Shopping Bag

A member of staff can bring in a bag of shopping and take the items out one by one. Put them all away again and then the group can try to remember as many items as possible.
This can lead on to a discussion about changing shopping habits, the affect of advertising etc.
The clients who are no longer shopping for themselves, will be astounded at the cost of everything.

Compile a collection of remembered sayings from Mothers, Fathers and Grandparents, for example;

'Make sure you wear clean underwear, you might be in an accident'.
'One hour before midnight is worth two afterwards'
'Don't let the sun go down on your wrath'

Ask the group "Do you think we received good advice?"

Compile A Quiz With A Theme

e.g. A ROYAL QUIZ

- Q. Name Queen Elizabeth's II children.
- A. Charles, Anne, Andrew and Edward.
  You might like to extend this question to include names of spouses and ex-spouses.

- Q. What date and where did Elizabeth's II coronation take place?
- A. 2nd June 1953 Westminster Abbey.

- Q. What famous horse race meeting does the royal family attend?
- A. Royal Ascot.

- Q. What happens on the Monarchs official birthday each year?
- A. Trooping of the Colour

- Q. How many previous Kings and Queens can you name?

- Q. Which King was executed by the parliamentarians?
- A. King Charles I

- Q. Which King is supposed to have burnt the cakes?
- A. King Alfred

- Q. Which rather large King had six wives?
- A. Henry VIII

Q. Can you name any of them and what was their fate?
A. Cathryn of Aragon (divorced), Anne Boleyn (beheaded), Jane Seymour(died), Anne of Cleeves(divorced),Cathryn Howard(beheaded), Cathryn Parr (Survived)

Q. Where are the Crown Jewels kept?
A. Tower of London.

Q. Can you think of any nursery rhymes with royal connection?
A.. e.g. Grand old Duke of York, Queen of Hearts, Old King Cole.

Q. Can you think of any songs with royal connections?
A. e.g. From Jack to a King. King of Road.

Q. What other countries can you name that have a royal family?
A. Spain, Monaco, Jordan.

Q. Name the Queen's London home.
A. Buckingham Palace.

Q. What happens when the Queen is in residence?
A. The Royal Standard is flying.

Q. Can you think of any films with royal connections?
A. The King and I, African Queen.

Q. Can you think of any local 'royal' street names?
A. e.g. Albert Rd.

This quiz could lead onto to a discussion on the benefits or otherwise in retaining the status of the present Royal Family.

Discussion Groups

"A mind that is stretched to a new idea never returns to it's original dimension."
Oliver Wendell Holmes

As mentioned previously the setting up and planning for any group is of paramount importance, and has been dealt with in the previous chapter.
We want to encourage social interaction between our clients whenever we can. A regular discussion group meeting with an agenda agreed by its members can be fun and stimulating for all its members, including the partially sighted and anyone for whom craft sessions can present difficulties.

A Suggestion For Getting Started

Looking at the Newspapers is a way of starting off a discussion. Both national and local news can be read aloud for everyone to voice their opinion on.

The Goings On With The Royal Family

Many older people have a fascination for royalty, often collecting newspaper cuttings, which can be made into a scrapbook. One lady living in a nursing home where I worked, read all she could about royalty in the newspapers, and wrote regularly to members of the Royal Family. She always had a reply, which she read out to her friends at mealtimes.

Horoscopes

The horoscope page is always a lot of fun. Which star sign is everyone? Do we believe that there is any truth in Astrology? Do we believe that anyone can foretell the future?

A Current Affairs Memory Game

This can be included in the current affairs discussion session, in order to exercise brains still further.

Newspaper pictures can be cut out and mounted.
Can anyone remember the personality?
Does anyone remember the story line?

Read aloud a headline.
Does anyone remember the article?

The crossword can be a group effort.

Newspaper activities can help to keep the group in touch with reality.

Health and Welfare Issues

Health Action Plan

With the help of a flip chart, if possible, try brainstorming with the group to produce a list of health considerations.
e.g. Diet, Dental Care, Footcare, Mobility, Leisure, Continence.

Try to avoid the session developing into an hour of individual complaints, but try to have a general discussion on positive ways in which elderly people can improve their health.

Case Studies Involving Welfare Rights And Support Organisations

Using a flip chart if possible, encourage the group to create a character or group of characters with problems.

e.g. A lady moves house to be near a relative. The relative dies and the lady feels isolated. What can she do to improve her situation?

or - An elderly gentleman can no longer care for himself, but does not feel yet that the time has come for him to enter a nursing home.
What services are available for him?
What advice could the group give?
Where would further advice be available from?

Reminiscence

Reminiscence is great fun and happens naturally and informally. We all enjoy talking over old times, when we bump into old friends. We often hang on to mementoes and take photographs to remind us of places and occasions.

Because we are aware that we have all had different experiences, this helps us to be aware of our unique identity, and raises self esteem. As everyone has memories to share, reminiscence allows everyone to feel equal.

To run a reminiscence group successfully, a leader is required who preferably, has had some training or experience in this field. An assistant who knows the group members well, gives support to the leader and the clients. Confused elderly clients may not always be able to express themselves verbally, but may still be recalling memories, as expressed by a wistful smile, tear on a cheek, or change in posture.

Reminiscence may be one of the few types of activity sessions that some clients participate in so its inclusion in the programme is very important.

Some clients may become distressed and will need support. Even happy memories can make us emotional.

Please refer to the information in previous chapter relating to setting up and running a group.

Benefits to Nursing and Care Staff

Reminiscence sessions have a definite benefit to Care Staff, as they are able to gain insight into the clients background and past achievements and learn from the clients experience. This helps a natural respect for the elderly person to grow and improves job satisfaction.

A care assistant can develop his or her role as a Keyworker, by being involved in Reminiscence.

The overall Care Plan can be prepared with a knowledge of the clients past lifestyle and past experience.

Equipment

Age Exchange and Age Concern England give information on training and equipment. The Winslow Press is a supplier offering a wide range of photographs, books, tapes, videos, slides and even smell kits.

You could start a collection of objects bought from junk shops, to bring out from time to time during the sessions.

My own collection bought mainly from car boot sales consists largely of household items including: a prosser, a flat iron, a last, old bottles, butter pats, a rag rug, a stone, hotwater bottle. I also have other items relating to the 20's, 30's and 40's like a gas mask from the second world war, some old money and an early typewriter etc.

The local folk museum may lend your centre or home same artifacts for a limited period. Staff may have some artifacts from their attics.

A display can be set up, involving the clients in the centre or home to act as a focal point for discussion.

Old photographs, newspapers and posters are especially useful to pass around the group to get the stories flowing. Maps, especially old ones can be spread out to help discussions about where people have lived, worked and travelled.

Suggested Topics and Cue Questions

Festivals	May Day, Carnivals, Any old photographs?
Christmas	How has Christmas changed over the years? Has anyone kept old cards or decorations?
School Days	Would some local school children like to visit and hear about the changes over the past 50 years in the lives of schoolchildren. Books? Equipment? Discipline? Uniform?
Childhood Games	Can we remember any of the games we played? Outings and holidays - Best things? Worst things? What food did we have? What clothes did we wear?
Courtship	What was allowed by parents in the past?
Health	Can anyone remember the old fashioned remedies? Having a baby - How have ideas changed?
Working Life	How has the working life of the nation changed? What types of work did women do in the past?
Shopping	How did we shop in the 40's? What did we buy? How much did we pay for basic items?
	Perhaps a member of staff could bring in a bag of shopping to jog memories and show how packaging has changed etc. Postcards, wrapping paper and calendars, using reproductions of old packaging can be passed round the group to help jog memories.
Wartime	Any photographs in uniform? What was it like living in London during the Blitz? What was is like serving in the Land Army? What items were rationed? Wartime weddings, how did people cope?
Entertainment	How has peoples leisure time changed?
Fashion	Has anyone any photographs?

More Reminiscence Activities

Some clients may like to start some scrap books. Local newspapers often publish photographs and articles depicting life as it was.

Everyone can keep a lookout for relevant photographs.

Music can reach everyone who can hear. A musical quiz playing short pieces of music from the past is a lot of fun and should end naturally with a sing song. Winslow Press can supply a tape for this purpose, or you could record your own.

A Reminiscence Quiz

A Quiz could be compiled, including questions about local history which should stimulate conversation. Do not rush through the quiz, but allow clients to reminisce. Here are some questions to start you off :

Q. Where did the local girl guides/boy scouts meet?

Q. Who sang "On the Good Ship Lollipop?"
A. Shirley Temple.

Chapter Two Mental Exercise

Q. Who was Wallace Simpson?
A. Edward VIII abdicated in order to marry twice divorced Wallace Simpson.

Q. Where was the nearest bomb to this centre dropped during the war?

Q. Who said "Come up and see me sometime?"
A. Mae West.

Q. Who said "Never in the field of human conflict was so much owed by so many to so few"?
A. Winston Churchill.

Q. Who was the first Prime Minister after World War II?
A. Clement Attlee.

Q. What year was our present queen crowned?
A. 1953.

Q. Who used to say "What's on the table Mabel?" and in which radio programme.
A. Wilfrid Pickles in 'Have a Go'.

Q. What was Gracie Fields' most popular song? Can you sing it?
A. "Sally."

Q. In what year did sweets come off ration?
A. 1953.

Q. Where was the nearest blacksmith to this Centre?

Q. What did the Rag and Bone Man give in exchange for peoples' unwanted goods?
A. Sometimes a goldfish, sometimes a balloon. Lime blocks for steps.

Q. How many old pennies to a pound?
A. 240.

Q. Where was the local cinema situated? And how much can you remember paying for admission.

Q. What year did the national health service come into operation.
A. 1948

Q. How have uniforms altered over the years?
A. Examples:
Nurses : No caps now. checked material, no stiff collars, plastic aprons.
Police : Badge on helmet now shiny, helmet usually replaced by flat cap, different style jacket.

Q. Which dances from the past can you name
A. e.g. Jitterbug, Military Two Step.

Chapter Two Mental Exercise

A Book of Memories

A keyworker and individual client could work on a 'Book of Memories', an activity which can be especially helpful for someone suffering with dementia. A scrapbook could be built up for photographs, cards and other personal memorabilia.

Another suggestion for a long term group project is to compile a collection of written memories and photographs, relating to a certain time, place or theme. If your home or centre has a long history, it would be an appropriate subject for a memory book. If most of your clients have lived their life in the locality of the centre, they may enjoy collating their knowledge in this way. This activity encourages reminiscence and communication, develops writing and graphics skills, and gives recognition to peoples lives.

The information can be reproduced into book form, with presentation to as high a standard as funds will allow. There follows a few pages from "Summer of 45" a book of memories of the end of World War Two, produced to mark the 50th anniversary of V.E. day compiled by The Young at Heart Club from the Forest of Dean. Apart from being an example of a group project, you may find the writings useful to read during reminiscence sessions.

Summer of 45

A collage of writings and photographs, representing the feel of life leading up to and including V.E. day 1945 as perceived fifty years later by members of the Young at Heart Club, Five Acres, Nr Coleford, Glos.

A new baby for V.E. Day

'I remember in the War, I was a young married woman then with young children. When the siren went, to warn us that there was an air raid, my husband would push the children and me in the cupboard under the stairs in case any bombs were dropped. Some of the older people would go up to the old tunnels belonging to Trafalgar park which served as an air raid shelter. We lived at Brierley at this time. I remember bombs dropped in the wood not far from Cannop Colliery. You could tell by the drone of the planes when it was Germany. On the wireless in the evening Lord Haw Haw would come on saying 'This is Germany calling Germany calling.' He then said where he thought the bombers would be over that night, and he was usually right in what he said. My husband worked at Cannop Colliery at the time. He was in the Homeguard and was called out at all hours at night.

My baby Daphne was born in April just before V.E. Day. In those days all babies were born at home and mothers stayed in bed for a fortnight. We had to use a chamber pot, as there were no inside toilets. Our tummies were bound for a fortnight to help keep our figures.

Babies were breast fed and left in their cots or prams in-between feeds which were strictly four hourly.'

Flora Mills

V.E. Day 1945

'My 13th birthday was approaching on V.E. day. Coincidentally my family and I were staying with my grandparents in Stratford-upon-Avon on the September day war was declared.

There was not a street party with food, but a general get together in the area.

A quartermaster naval petty officer on leave at the time had 'acquired' a mortar which he felt was appropriate to fire. Thinking he could enhance the effect, the PO placed the lit mortar in a metal dustbin and put on the lid.

There was a huge bang but people were very surprised when after what seemed a whole minute the lid clattered to earth. Fortunately no-one was hurt but peace in Europe for us certainly came in with a bang.'

Monica Weighell

My Memories of the Forest of Dean in Wartime

'VE day here was jubilant - great news after six years wait that had marred so many lives.

It was comparatively quiet as regards to bombing etc. The woods were taken over by American Forces and also our own army engineers. Broadwell was made into a Prisoner of War Camp, containing both German and Italians. Some of these have never returned to their own Country, but have married and live locally.

My husband, having been a forestry worker, was transferred to the War Agricultural Department. He took lorry loads of prisoners to work at farms in Herefordshire - quite a trying job in the black out, driving small roads with only a small slit of light from the head lamps.

Many other people including myself worked twelve hour shifts at Hereford Munitions. We worked from 6am - 6pm for two weeks, then from 6pm to 6am for two weeks. Wages were £3 to £3.50 per week. I found it very rough having been a shop assistant in a large shop of that time - Trotters, in Coleford. The factory was bombed only once. Several people were killed, including one local, Mr E Gwilliam (Ted).

We often watched flares and bombs lighting up Bristol, the centre of which was being completely demolished.

On V.E. day 8th May, my husbands 28th birthday, we went to the officers quarters at the P.O.W. camp. We had a great time - plenty of food and most had too much to drink. A great time until early morning. Although we had lots of food on V.E. day, rationing of some goods lasted until 1955-56.'

Olive Williams

Chapter Two Mental Exercise

More Memories of the End of the War

'I remember the relief of no more bombs, no more dreading the sirens for I lived in Bristol and we were really heavily bombed. I was married in March 1945 at the age of 19 years old and in the summer of '45 found my husband in Italy. He was a navigator pilot with the Royal Air Force.

My job was in a local grocer shop, doling out the meagre rations and keeping special rare items of food (such as fruit cake) under the counter for our regular customers. Clothes were still unobtainable without coupons unless you had plenty of money to buy them on the black market. Shoes with wooden soles were not on coupons and were surprisingly comfortable.

As a shop assistant - I am the tall one

My husband Bert

My weekends and two evenings a week were taken up with 'The Girls Training Corps'. We learned to march and do plane spotting and on Saturday evenings and Sunday afternoons we served Tea and played records for the forces stationed in Bristol, all nationalities. We were all girls who for one reason or another couldn't go into the forces and felt we were helping out a bit. Actually the navy and white uniform was quite smart and those of us who went on to join the Royal Observer Corps had a lovely grey and Airforce blue uniform. Two of my friends met their husbands through the G.T.C. Our marching tune was 'Blaze Away' the words started - 'We are the G.T.C. of Bristol and we'll help to win the war.' Anyway summer of '45 saw all this coming to an end although I did start my own company of G.T.C. when I came to Coleford to live in 1947.'

Jean - a refugee from the occupied channel islands, in the uniform of the Girls Training Corp.

Lillian N. Howell

30

Chapter Two Mental Exercise

have you an old mackintosh?

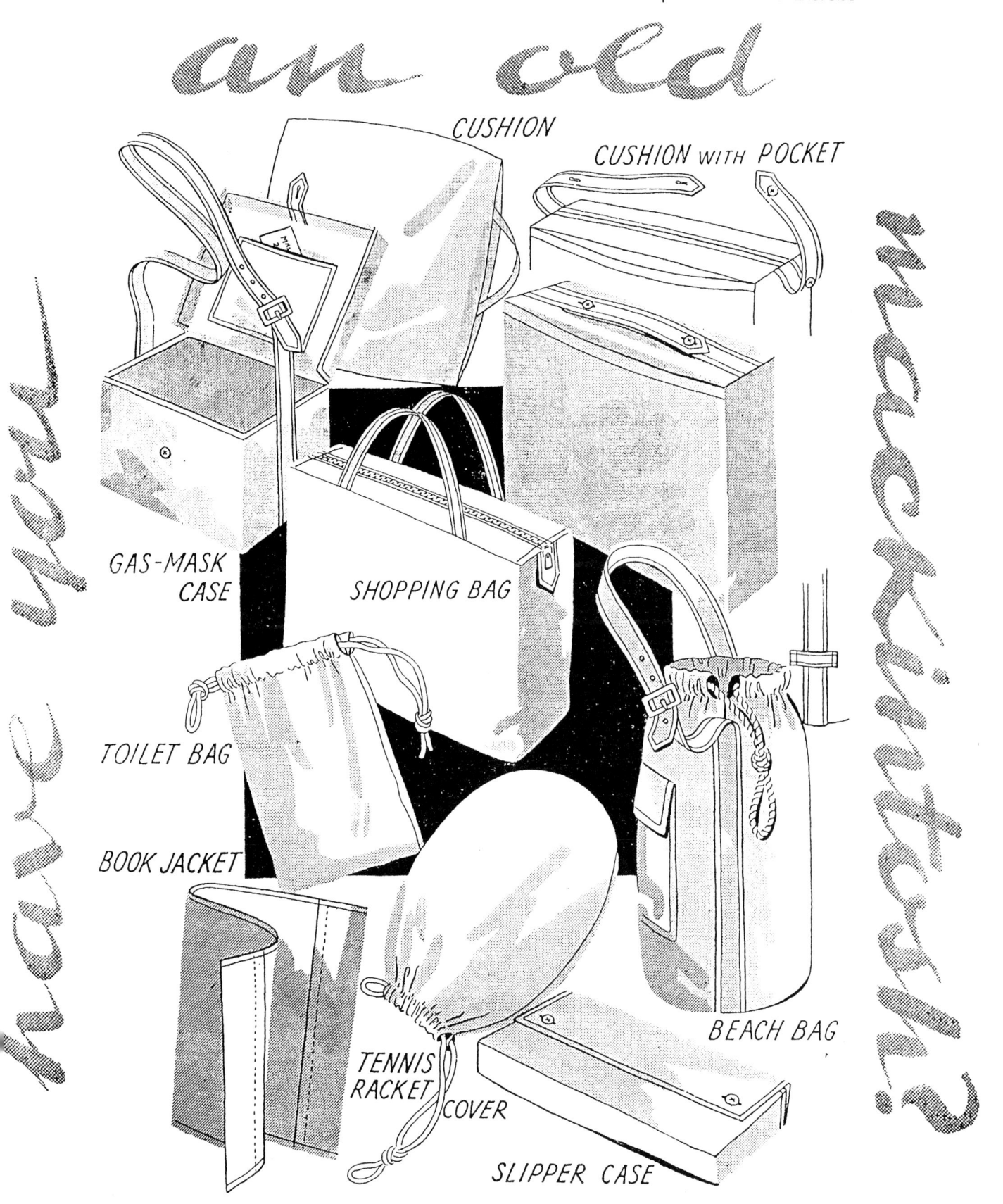

CUSHION
CUSHION with POCKET
GAS-MASK CASE
SHOPPING BAG
TOILET BAG
BOOK JACKET
TENNIS RACKET COVER
BEACH BAG
SLIPPER CASE

HOW often have you hung up an old raincoat in a corner, and left it for many moons, saying, "I can't wear this any longer, but it's much too good to throw away!" Actually, an old mackintosh should be treated with great respect, as it is invaluable for such things as book-jackets, racket covers, toilet bags—in fact there is no limit to the amount of useful things you can make. Perhaps the family all need new gas-mask cases?

Chapter Two Mental Exercise

An Eventful Year

'I remember 1945. I was roped in (almost literally) to help to ring the church bells. As instructed I jerked the woolly grip on the bell rope and stretched upward. Looking down, I saw surprised faces watching me rise towards a small hole in the ceiling. I travelled quite quickly back to the floor after I released my grip on the rope.

I remember May. The victory in Europe. The streets of Doncaster were full of strangers, united in feelings of joy, relief and disbelief. It was a time of general celebration (and not a drunk in sight).

That year I had my first experience of hospitals. Needing an urgent minor operation, my mother and I had to visit (walking two miles) the local official of a scheme which would entitle me to treatment. We had to fill in forms and pay a subscription before we had permission to go ahead with necessary arrangements.

They seemed the longest four days of my life, in a ward for twenty women, between one who was stone deaf and another who could be heard outside. I was confined to bed, not allowed to read, with no radio and visiting hours were strictly adhered to. My friends who came to visit me during their lunch hour were not allowed in to cheer me up.

We had two anatomy lessons at the hospital, but they did not continue because the school could not afford to pay the teaching sister. We had no craft or cookery rooms, and no science laboratory. Our games of hockey and rounders were played in the local public park.

I remember food rationing. We had no bananas, cream or fizzy drinks; there were few sweets, chocolates or biscuits; and tea, coffee, milk, sugar, eggs, meat and even sausages were scarce. They were too precious to allow incompetent children to experiment with cooking. Clothing coupons had to be saved for essentials, even when leaving home to go to college.

I remember my first room at the all girls' college. It was a tiny unheated and draughty triangular cupboard under the stairs. After three days in bed, almost immobile with a painful stiff neck (an auspicious start to a Physical Education course) a change of room was arranged. This was in the main building which had one staircase. The Vice Principal had a room on the first floor and any visitors were introduced to her as a matter of courtesy. The Principals' room overlooked the main entrance. She was a forbidding lady, with dark hair pulled back into a bun, who regularly preached at the Cathedral.

Twice a week there was a formal evening meal for which we had a rota, naming the lucky girls who were to sit at the Top Table. A daunting prospect as forbidden topics for conversation were the weather, politics and personalities. One evening each week we were expected to attend the Chapel Practice. The outer doors of the building were locked at 9.30pm on weekdays, 10.00pm on Saturdays and a book was signed for weekend passes.

Our only recreations were swimming at the local baths, team matches on Saturdays, the cinema maybe twice a term (many students had repayable loans) and portable radios with heavy rechargeable batteries, if you were lucky.

I was fortunate because I was able to visit a friend of my aunt's for Sunday tea, and enjoy the luxury of ham sandwiches, tinned fruit and cake. She was grateful for the kindness shown to her when she had been evacuated with her children. They were teenagers, before those aged 13 to 19 were identified as a special group, and we would cycle to the Derbyshire dales or attend the evening church service.

Travelling was not easy. A visit home took five hours - a journey by train and two buses. With petrol rationed, our modest Morris 8 could only manage one outing a month. On a steep gradient passengers had to walk to the top of the hill and in freezing fog we raised the windscreen. I learned to drive on virtually empty roads.

Although French was one of our subjects we had no opportunity to visit France or chat up French boys. Our only contact was a student from Guernsey who had survived starvation during the occupation.

I should have been Mary in the Nativity Play that year had not a nasty bout of 'flu and a cough intervened. Instead of Christmas festivities, a large group of us were treated to two aspirins every four hours. We went home for the holidays two days late, and had to return a day early to do the exams we had missed. These were to decide our suitability to continue the course. Despite the privations, we did survive, and enjoyed the comradeship and sense of adventure.'

Barbara Jenkins

War Memories

'I was ten years old when war was declared. I commenced my 'secondary' education at Lydney Grammar School in 1940, and because of the Battle of Britain the school year started in mid-August instead of the previously announced date - 12.9.40. For a while we also shared the school with pupils from Yorkly in Birmingham when their school was evacuated. We used it in the mornings (including Saturdays) and the Yorkly pupils in the afternoons.

Because of food rationing people were encouraged to make their own jam. The Women's Institute movement was allowed sugar for this purpose - fruit was 'collected' and school kitchens were used during the holidays. I remember being the youngest 'cook' at one jam-making session at Yorkly school kitchens. The jams had to go to shops to be sold (against the points' which were allowed for such purposes). The jar labels wore the W.I. crest. It was, of course, just like home-made. I remember having time off school to collect rose-hips. These were used to produce rose-hip syrup which was issued (together with concentrated orange juice) to ensure that wartime values had all the necessary vitamins.

My father, being too old for national service, was a warden with the local Air Raid Precaution (A.R.P). They used an old cottage for their base which was 'Manned' nightly. I received the princely sum of 1/- (one shilling or 5p in decimal coinage) for clearing the cottage on a Saturday morning. It had an old-fashioned open fireplace in which they had massive coal fires. Lots of ashes and dust!

From the American servicemen who were in the area we learnt that they ate grey squirrel (much as we did rabbits). Why not us, we thought? The skins were very hard to remove but once achieved the flesh was a delicate pink and resembled a young rabbit. Cooking in a casserole the taste was a cross between rabbit and chicken. Quite a delicacy.'

Hilda Jones

Chapter Two Mental Exercise

Womens Forestry Service

'We were the young women employed by the Forestry Commission. We worked alongside the men on Highmeadow estate from 1940-1946. We were issued with dark green overalls and a green metal badge with the crown circled with the words 'Womens Forestry Service Forestry Commission'.

Although we have never been recognised as an army service our work was of national importance. We cleared and planted thousands of acres of trees, all conifers and broadleaf, also nursery work, and sawing pit props. Fifty years on, thousands of tourists enjoy the scenic walks through our forest. Our V.E. and V.J. celebrations were held in the English Bicknor Village Hall.'

Liz Cook

'I married in 1940 and stopped work, as women usually did after marriage. My wedding bouquet contained bronze chrysanths and asparagus fern, and the dress was blue. I celebrated V.E. Day at a Dance in Aston Ingham Village Hall.'

Rose Taylor

War memories

'My earliest war memory is that of going into our neighbours' shelter each night in anticipation of air-raids on the Austin factory in Birmingham., some miles away from my home. Subsequently we had a steel table shelter which was elegantly covered with an Indian cotton bedspread which would be removed when friends and I gave 'concerts' using the table-top as a stage. It made a lovely noise if we 'tap-danced' on it!

To my mother's horror, the local greengrocers would sell us children ½d or 1d carrots - unwashed but lovely to crunch in place of sweets.

One afternoon at school the siren went and we were leaded sedately across the playground towards the brick-built shelter with a re-enforced concrete roof, when two German bombers flew very low overhead. They dropped one bomb on the railway line near the Austins and I think this was the only one during the whole of the war. One elevation of the factory was painted to look like a row of terraced houses and it was years before the camouflage peeled off. The school shelter also doubled as changing rooms for P.E.

My father, at 37 in the reserved occupation of teaching and whose eyesight was below standard, was in the Red Cross and he has many stories to tell of going into the city centre after a raid. One night he went into a communal shelter and was confronted with a load of people whose heads seemed to be floating well above their shoulders. We wondered what kind of bomb could cause this. On further investigation we realised that it was a group of Sikhs whose turbans had showed up in the half-light but whose dark-skinned faces we could not see.

After D-day many wounded service personnel came to local hospitals and were a common sight in their bright blue uniforms.

It was the young people's great joy when an American troop train went by because they threw sweets, magazines and chewing gum on to the embankment and we then quickly retrieved it, oblivious to approaching trains.

My standard breakfast was a dried egg 'pancake' which I didn't really like but I knew my mother had given up her ration so that I could be fed. She never did eat breakfast again, having given up during the war.

I was 13 when I was confirmed and my dress was made from a length of parachute silk, nefariously obtained by a friend of my fathers. Dealing in off-ration goods was quite clandestine. Recently I was told of the owner of a corner shop who dealt extensively in black market food. She was sold a cheese which was so 'far gone' is was runny, so she packed it up and took it on two buses, back to the people who had sold it to her.

My memory is strong of an overwhelming feeling of camaraderie and willingness to help anyone, friend or stranger - something not quite so apparent today?'

Monica Weighell

Chapter Two Mental Exercise

War Time recipes

Suet Pastry
1lb flour and 1 teaspoon Baking Powder
½ teaspoon salt
4oz suet
Water to mix

Mix flour, salt and baking powder. Shred and grate or chop the suet finely. Mix with the flour then add water to make a fairly stiff paste. Roll out and use to make a savoury or sweet roll or use to make dumplings for a vegetable stew.

Bacon Roly Poly
Scrape the bacon from bacon bones after cooking. Mix with cooked onions and mixed herbs. Roll in suet pastry. Tie in pudding cloth and cook in boiling pan up to 2 hours.

Apple Roly Poly
Cut up apples. Place on suet pastry with dried fruit and a little syrup or treacle or jam. Roll up in pudding cloth and cook in boiling pan.

Dumplings
Add chopped cooked onion, herbs and pepper to basic mix. Make into balls. Add to stews or casseroles or alternatively use as a pie crust for a vegetable pie to which you have added a sauce flavoured with an oxo cube. Tinned vegetables can also be used in this way.

Wood Fowl Casserole
1 Young Rabbit
Onions
Clarified fat or margarine
Flour
Water
Salt and pepper, Sage

Paunch and skin the rabbit and cut into joints. Place fat in frying pan and cook rabbit until browned, turning frequently.
Remove and place in casserole dish
Cook off the onions in the pan then drain and add to casserole. Add flour to frying pan to take up the fat and cook through to brown, adding water to make a gravy. Season and add to casserole with crumbled sage. Place in a slow oven until well cooked.
Vegetables may be added to the casserole or cooked and served separately.

Savoury Pudding
1lb stale bread
Medium to Large Onion
Sage, Thyme and Parsley
2-3oz Margarine or Grated Suet
Teaspoon of Marmite, yeast extract or 1 oxo cube
1 Tablespoon Dried Egg Powder
2 Tablespoons Water

Soak bread then squeeze out excess moisture. Meanwhile chop onion and cook off in small amount of water. Stir bread, onions, herbs and margarine together. Add reconstituted egg or 1 fresh egg and yeast extract or oxo cube.
Place in greased pie dish and cook in moderate oven.
Serve with a well flavoured gravy as an alternative to meat for a hearty lunch.

War and Peace Pudding
1 cup each of the following:
  Flour, breadcrumbs, grated raw potato and grated raw carrots.
½ cup each of:
  Suet or grated margarine
  Dried fruit
2 teaspoons bicarbonate of soda
½ cup of water

Mix all together. Place in a greased basin. Cover and steam for two hours. Serve hot with a suitable sauce.

This recipe came from Canada where it had been developed during the first world war.

Janet Marrott

Chapter Three Song And Verse

Rationale

Singing in a group brings a feeling of togetherness, brings back memories and often stimulates laughter.

It is impossible to please everyone, but this is the one activity that pleases almost everyone, and does not require mobility.

It is important to include familiar songs, which can evoke memories, and to encourage any group member to tell a background story surrounding a song, which gives relevance to their life.

Include hymns, because Sunday School was an important part of most elderly peoples childhood.

Poetry can reach peoples deepest feelings and in a group situation, encourages the sharing of emotions.

Singing

Large print song books, hymn books and sing-a-long tapes are available from music shops and specialist suppliers.

Encourage clients to sit in a semi-circle, if possible, so that people can relate to one another more easily during conversation.

Many elderly people will know the words off by heart once prompted by the first line and tune.

Ask around for any favourite choices.

Some centres are lucky enough to have someone to play the piano.

Here are some well know traditional songs and Hymns to start you off. I find that often, it works better if the less well known verses are left out.

All Things Bright And Beautiful

Chorus.
All things bright and beautiful,
All creatures great and small,
All things wise and wonderful,
The Lord God made them all.

Each little flower that opens,
Each little bird that sings,
He made their glowing colours,
He made their tiny wings.

The purple - headed mountain,
The river running by,
The sunset in the morning
That brightens up the sky.

He gave us eyes to see them,
And lips that we might tell
How great is God Almighty
Who has made all things well.

Onward Christian Solders

Onward Christian Solders,
Marching as to war,
With the Cross of Jesus,
Going on before.
Christ the royal Master,
Leads against the foe;
Forward into battle,
See his banner go.

Onward Christian Solders,
Marching as to war,
With the Cross of Jesus
Going on before.

Onward then ye people,
Join our happy throng,
Blend with ours your voices
In the triumph song.
glory, laud and honour,
Unto Christ the King.
This through countless ages
Men and angels sing.

Onward Christian solders etc.

Lead us, heavenly father lead us

Lead us, heavenly father lead us
O'er the worlds tempestuous sea
Guard us, guide us, keep us, feed us
For we have no help but thee
yet possessing every blessing,
if our God our Father be.

Spirit of our God descending
Fill our hearts with heavenly joy
Love with every passion blending
Pleasure that can never die
Thus provided, pardoned, guided,
Nothing can our peace destroy,

Traditional Songs

She'll Be Coming Round The Mountain

She'll be coming round the mountain when she comes,
She'll be coming round the mountain when she comes,
She'll be coming round the mountain,
Coming round the mountain,
Coming round the mountain,
Coming round the mountain when she comes.

She'll be driving six white horses when she comes etc.

Daisy Daisy

Daisy, Daisy,
Give me your answer do,
I'm half crazy,
All for the love of you,
It won't be a stylish marriage,
I can't afford a carriage.
But you'll look sweet, upon the seat,
Of a bicycle made for two.

London's Burning - A Round

London's burning, London's burning.
Fetch the engines, Fetch the engines.
Fire, Fire, Fire, Fire,
Pour on water, Pour on water.

One Man Went To Mow

One man went to mow,
Went to mow a meadow,
One man and his dog,
Went to mow a meadow.

Two men went etc.

Early One Morning

Early one morning,
Just as the sun was rising,
I heard a maid singing in the valley below,
Oh don't deceive me, Oh never leave me,
How could you use such a poor maiden so?

My Grandfathers Clock

My grandfathers clock was too large for the shelf,
So it stood ninety years on the floor;
It was taller by half than the old man himself
Though it weighed not a pennyweight more.
It was bought on the morn of the day that he was born,
And was always his treasure and pride;
But it stopped short, never to go again
When the old man died.

Chorus: Ninety years without slumbering tick, tock, tick, tock,
His life seconds numbering tick, tock, tick, tock
It stopped short never to go again
When the old man died.

In watching its pendulum swing to and fro,
Many hours had he spent while a boy;
And in childhood and manhood the clock seemed to know
And to share both his grief and his joy.
For it struck twenty-four when he entered at the door,
With a blooming and beautiful bride;
But it stopped short, never to go again
When the old man died.

It rang an alarm in the dead of the night,
An alarm that for years had been dumb;
And we knew that his spirit was pluming for flight
That his hour of departure had come.
Still the clock kept the time, with a soft and muffled chime
As we silently stood by its side;
But it stopped short, never to go again
When the old man died.

Poetry

Hunt around in most homes and you will find a poetry book, even if it has remained unopened since it's owner was a child. In recent years an interest in poetry has become more popular and an anthology is usually on the Best Seller List at Christmas time.

Many elderly people remember reciting poems at school, and will often join in with relish if reminded of a familiar first line, by William Wordsworth, Rudiyard Kipling and many others. An elderly lady in one of my groups said that she had been in a "Speaking Choir" at school and really enjoyed reciting familiar poems and many that were completely new to everyone.

A humorous poem by Pam Ayres will have everyone laughing and remind individuals of amusing rhymes they have learnt in the past.

The group may like to discuss how they feel about a particular poem or what ideas the poet might have been trying to convey to us.

If the interest within the group grows, some members may like to try writing down thoughts of their own. The local College of Further Education will be able to advise should the Group want a qualified teacher.

A flip chart is useful when composing a group poem, which can take two or more sessions to produce and gives clients something to explore mentally between times. Local newspapers regularly print poems sent in by local amateur poets.

This poem by Joan North expresses her feelings whilst a patient on an elderly care ward in hospital.

What impressions does the group receive from the poem?

Geriatric Ward

Tottering steps and Zimmer frames slowly cross the floor,
Such fragile figures so determined to reach their goal;
The struggle to put on a dressing gown,
To reach a faraway object on the bedside table;
Patient endurance and closed eyes. How still and quiet,
Full of unspoken sympathy for each other.
Bright kindly nurses in and out, looking so young;
Urging the impossible - to drink more, eat more.
Visitors come in bringing the world and friendship.
Patients' faces lighten. They rouse themselves.
Then quiet again.

There is love in this ward,
Some clumsiness of communication,
And unimaginative treatment,
But mostly love I think.

Some very famous classic poems

The Daffodils

I wander'd lonely as a cloud
That floats on high o'er vales and hills,
When all at once I saw a cloud,
A host of golden daffodils,
Beside the lake, beneath the trees
Fluttering and dancing in the breeze.

Continuous as the stars that shine
And twinkle on the milky way,
They stretched in never ending line
Along the margin of a bay;
Ten thousand saw I at a glance
Tossing their heads in sprightly dance.

The waves beside them danced, but they
Out-did the sparkling waves in glee;
A Poet could not but be gay
In such jocund company !
I gazed and gazed but little thought
What wealth the show to me had brought;

For oft, when on my couch I lie
In vacant or in pensive mood,
They flash upon that inward eye
Which is the bliss of solitude;
And then my heart with pleasure fills,
And dances with the daffodils.
           William Wordsworth

The Eagle

He clasps the crag with crooked hands,
Close to the sun in lonely lands,
Ring'd with the azure world, he stands.
The wrinkled sea beneath him crawls,
He watches from his mountain walls,
And like a thunderbolt he falls.

     Alfred, Lord Tennyson

Past And Present

I remember, I remember
The house where I was born,
The little window where the sun
Came peeping in at morn;
He never came a wink too soon
Nor brought too long a day;
But now, I often wish the night
Had borne my breath away.

I remember ,I remember
The roses, red and white,
The violets, and the lily-cups,
Those flowers made of light.
The lilacs where the robin built,
And where my brother set
The laburnum on his birthday,
The tree is living yet.

I remember, I remember
Where I was used to swing,
And thought the air must rush as fresh
To swallows on the wing;
My spirit flew in feathers then
That is so heavy now,
And summer pools could hardly cool
The fever on my brow.

I remember, I remember
The fir-trees dark and high,
I used to think their slender tops
Were close against the sky;
It was a childish ignorance,
But now 'tis little joy
To know I'm farther off from Heaven
Than when I was a boy.
            Thomas Hood

Chapter Four Arts and Crafts

Rationale

The aim of craft activity is to allow clients to express themselves, build confidence and self-esteem and have fun through the use of colour, shape, texture and the experience of creating a valued product.

In my opinion one cannot over estimate the therapeutic value of creativity, as we concentrate our minds, develop ideas, and soothe away negative thoughts (or channel them into our creation).

Clients may not have had the opportunity or confidence in the past to attend classes, so the introduction of a craft session into the centre or home may build that confidence. In time a client may feel sufficiently confident to attend a college class.

Chapter Four Arts and Crafts

Simple Jewellery Making - Beads

From the earliest times, people have wanted to adorn themselves with attractive objects. This activity should encourage lots of discussion and, perhaps, the clients may show their personal jewellery to the group, discussing the history behind each piece.

Many of the clients with failing eyesight will not be able to manage this activity. But, it has proved so popular with some clients and staff that I have included it. As well as papier-mâché, the group can make beads from clay or salt dough.

Project - Papier-mâché Beads

Materials and Equipment

Decorative paper - e.g. gift wrapping paper, shiny pages from magazines, marbleised paper etc.
A long ruler.
Scissors.
Pencil or pen.
Wallpaper paste and container.
Cocktail sticks.
Petroleum jelly.

Method

Make up wallpaper paste
Coat end cocktail sticks with petroleum jelly.
Using ruler, pen and scissors, produce very narrow, elongated triangles, approximately 1cm. at the base stretching to about 10 cm. or more.
Coat the back of each triangle with paste.
Carefully wind the paper around a cocktail stick, starting at the base of the triangle.
Leave to dry overnight.
Remove the beads and varnish if desired.

The beads can be used for earrings, necklaces etc. Components (called findings) to make up earrings, brooches etc. can be bought from craft shops.
Large beads made from thicker paper can be used to make chunkier necklaces or even bead curtains.

Project - Clay Beads

Some of the earliest beads were made when Early Man noticed small hard pieces of clay in his camp fire.

The benefits to the elderly clients in working with clay are mentioned elsewhere. In making these beads, the hands and fingers really get some exercise and the end product gives a lot of satisfaction.

Materials and Equipment

A small quantity of red earthenware clay - from a craft supplier, or a local potter. (The clay needs to be kept in an air tight container, wrapped in polythene)
A paintbrush handle or other tool to make holes in the clay

Method

Remove air from clay by kneading.
Roll and shape beads.
Make marks in beads, if desired, for decoration.
Make holes for threading.
Leave beads to dry slowly.
The appearance of the beads will be improved if they are polished from time to time during the drying period, with the hands. (This technique is called burnishing.)
The beads can be fired in a simple sawdust kiln, or even the hottest part of a domestic fire.

How to make a Sawdust Kiln From a Biscuit Tin[2]

This will enable you to fire beads and other small clay objects.

Equipment

A large square biscuit tin punched with small regular holes along the sides (approx. 6 a side.) - (No lid).
Sawdust.
Firelighters and matches.

Method - An outside activity!!

Ask everyone to stand back
Fill tin with sawdust and put on the ground
Bury bone dry clay beads (and any other tiny clay items)
Lay the two firelighters on the sawdust and light
The firelighters will flare up at first, then the sawdust will smoulder and the firing will take about 8 hours
When cool the beads can be threaded onto leather thongs, and made into necklaces.

---

[2] Acknowledgement to Sara Weaving

Chapter Four Arts and Crafts

Pottery

The experience of handling and creating using clay is such a therapeutic experience that it is worth going to some trouble to provide this opportunity to a well established craft group.
Although self-hardening clay is available from craft shops, there is nothing quite like the natural clay that you can obtain from craft suppliers or perhaps from a local professional potter.
Your local college may be able to put you in touch with a pottery teacher, who would come to your centre to give a demonstration and advise, for a fee.

Project - a slip decorated thumb pot

Over three sessions

This activity may be messy, but it is easier than you may expect to produce an attractive result.

Materials And Equipment

A suitable quantity of red earthenware clay. Ask your supplier for advice on quantity, which will depend on the number of pots required.
A small quantity of coloured slip (liquid clay).
A small quantity of transparent glaze.
Fern leaves to produce a design.
Soft brushes.
Small pieces of sponge.
A small sharp knife.
A suitable large tray or board to store pots on.

Method - First Session

First the clay must be wedged to remove any air bubbles, by banging the clay onto the table and kneading it with the heel of the hand.
Cut in half to check on air bubbles.
Grasp a ball of clay in your left hand (if you are right handed), whilst the thumb of the right hand is pressed into the centre.
The ball is then rotated whilst the thumb squeezes from the inside to the required shape. The walls and base must not be too thick.
Smooth off with a damp sponge.

Decoration

Lay a leaf or leaves inside or on the outside of the pot.
Paint on the slip with a brush.
Leave for 2 to 3 hours.
Peel off the leaf leaving the sharp design of the leaf.
Dry the pot very slowly over several days (spray with water to delay drying).

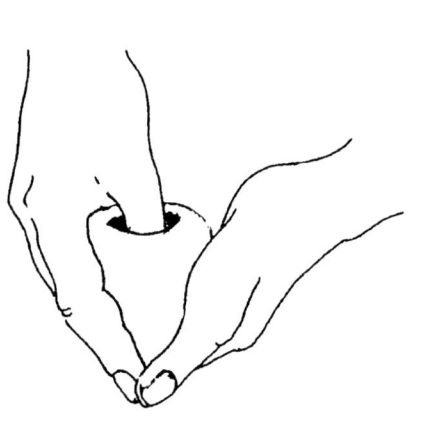

Method -Second Session

Once the pot is Leather Hard the bottom of the pot can be tidied up with a knife and damp sponge

When the pot is completely dry it is ready for its first firing in a kiln.
A local professional potter or college may perform this service for a fee.

Method - Third Session

When the pot has been fired once it will need to be dipped in a suitable transparent glaze.
Wipe the bottom with a damp sponge to prevent the glaze sticking to the kiln shelf. Try not to touch the glazed pot too much.
The pot now goes for its final glaze firing.

Other methods of decoration include:
Pushing objects into the soft clay to leave an impression and glazing.
Trailing the slip onto the pot, and glazing.
Omitting the slip and using one of the many ready mixed glazes instead of the transparent one.

Water Colour Painting

Many people take up painting when they retire, and find that this new hobby enriches their lives enormously. One of my group members tried her first painting at the age of ninety-three!

Not only are new skills developed, and new friends made at group painting sessions, but awareness of colours and shapes in the environment is heightened.

Basic Materials

Cartridge paper sketch pad for the first attempts.
A water colour pad - A3 size at least.
A starter set of student water colour tubes of paint.
Large and small soft brushes.
An old plate to use as a palate.
Absorbent paper for cleaning.
A container for water.

Method

A suggestion to get you started with colour mixing.

Squeeze a little paint of each colour onto the palate.
Cut long coloured strips from a glossy magazine.
Stick a strip across a page of the sketch book.
Beside each colour along the strip, paint onto the adjacent paper, extending the colours of the section of magazine.
Practise mixing the colours to match the coloured areas from the magazine in this way, washing the brush often in clean water.

Perhaps next session the group may like to try painting from a vase of flowers or simple still life.

Points To Remember For Painting Sessions

- A member of staff joining in, with their own work, is very helpful. (If he or she does not try to influence the subject matter of the clients work)

- Try to maintain a quiet atmosphere for as long as possible.

- Never laugh at the results or say 'I am not artistic'.

- Keep the water for washing brushes very clean or the colours will become muddy.

- If the group decide to keep their work to display it, a card mount helps to make the work look good (never write names on paintings reminiscent of primary school). Ask the client to sign their work.

- Try to encourage clients to put their own personality into their work. (A camera can record exactly what is there.)

- An overall design is just as worthy as a conventional viewpoint of a still life and can be more creative in approach.

Therapeutic Painting Sessions

Sometimes, the end result of creativity can become completely unimportant, as is the case with a group painting session viewed purely as a means of relaxation, or as a means of communicating feelings. The painting or paintings can be retained if the clients choose to do so.

Materials and Equipment

Large sheets of good quality cartridge paper.
Very large sheets so that everyone can work on together, are difficult to obtain, but try a printers.
Water colour paper is wonderful to paint on, but much more expensive.
Fluid paint -'clear powder paint' is an inexpensive highly concentrated water colour and an excellent choice. (Available from educational suppliers, including Nottingham Rehab.)
Large and small brushes.
Lots of jam jars for paints and for washing brushes.

Method

A quiet room must be found where it will be possible to have an hour or so with no interruptions.
Gentle music playing in the background helps the atmosphere.
The room should be well prepared with all equipment laid out in advance.
For a theme perhaps someone could read a poem, or the painting could be related to the music.
It may take some minutes before everyone is engrossed in their painting, but during a successful session the benefits can be enormous
At the end of the session the painting or paintings can be discarded or retained as wished by the clients.
Some time should be allowed at the end for discussion and winding down. As the group meeting becomes established as a regular event, trust can build up, allowing clients to feel less self-conscious about painting along side others in a spontaneous way.

If you wish to explore therapeutic art groups further, I would recommend "Art therapy for groups" by Marian Liebman.

Dough Craft

This craft has the advantage that the ingredients are easily obtainable and inexpensive. The clients fingers are given lots of exercise, and the end results are reliably good which raises self esteem.

Materials

Twice as much in volume of plain flour as salt
e.g. two mugs of flour to one mug of salt.
Warm water and a few drops of oil to mix.
Mixing bowl.
Useful tools: e.g. knives, a rolling pin, garlic press (for hair).
Items such as bits of twig, cloves etc. can be added for decoration.
Possibly - Food colouring.
Water based paints.
Varnish.

Method

Mix dough as if making pastry.
Knead dough very thoroughly and then mould as required.
Moisten parts to connect.
A paper clip can be pushed in at this stage to aid hanging.
Dry the modelled dough on a baking sheet in a warm place.
Bake in an oven on a very low heat for approximately 4/6 hours until baked hard. The heat can be gradually increased. To decorate, food colouring can be added in the mixing, or paint after baking with water based paint.
Varnish will protect and add sheen.

Suggestions For Projects

Candlesticks - cut a ring to fit a candle base and decorate with leaves and roses.
Make the leaves and roses in the way that you would to decorate an apple pie, i.e. a thin strip rolled up makes a rose, leaf shaped pieces can have veins added with a knife.

Brooches - cut shapes and fix a safety pin in the back before you bake.

Make a flat basket shape with a handle to hang on the wall. Make lattice marks in the dough. Once it is baked, varnish it and decorate by gluing on small dried flowers.

Christmas tree decorations can be made by using biscuit cutters in the shapes of bells, angels etc. and then pushing in small pieces of foil.

Decorating Paper - Marbling

Materials And Equipment

Rubber gloves.
A Shallow container e.g. redundant meat tin.
3/4 jam jars.
A few tubes of oil paint.
White Spirit (non toxic is available from good art shops).
Paper cut to container size.
Paint brushes.
Newspaper.

Method

Protect furniture and wear rubber gloves.
Open window.
Half fill container with water and a dash of spirit.
Mix a squirt of oil paint with a little spirit in each of the jam jars.
Drop two or three colours onto the water swirl gently with the paint brushes.
Lay a piece of paper onto the surface of the water and paint.
Lift off marbled paper, hold up for every one to admire and lay on newspaper to dry.

* A more controlled method involves using carragheen moss, available from craft suppliers. This produces a clear jelly like surface, so that the colour can be moved around into a static pattern

For using in a confined space- commercial marbleising ink can be bought from craft suppliers which is completely free of any fumes.

Decorating Paper - Monoprinting

Many famous artists have used the monoprint technique. For a group who would like to have a go at a more experimental creative activity, monoprinting is ideal.

Materials and Equipment

Water based printing ink if possible, otherwise thick ready-mixed paint works well. A dark colour seems to work best.
A Smooth surface-plate glass if possible or a Formica topped table will do.
A Rubber printing roller.
Good quality cartridge paper.

Method

Protect furniture
Squeeze paint onto glass and roller. Practise will show you how much, but it is important not to have too much paint.
Unless you want an all over design, the centre can be cut out of one piece of paper leaving a narrow surround to act as a stencil. This can produce a masked area around your print which gives it a professional finish.
Lay this surround on the inked smooth surface.
Draw into exposed inked area with fingers, brush or use any thing which produces a different kind of mark.
Lay paper down next and press all over with hand.
Peel off the paper and you will have a Monoprint.

Chapter Four Arts and Crafts

More Printmaking - Leaf Prints

Materials And Equipment

A variety of leaves.
Ready-mixed paint.
Paper.
A4 size plain card (for Greeting cards).
Brushes.

Method

Protect furniture.
Apply paint (not too much) to underside of leaves, where veins are raised up.
Press onto paper or card with newspaper and lift off.

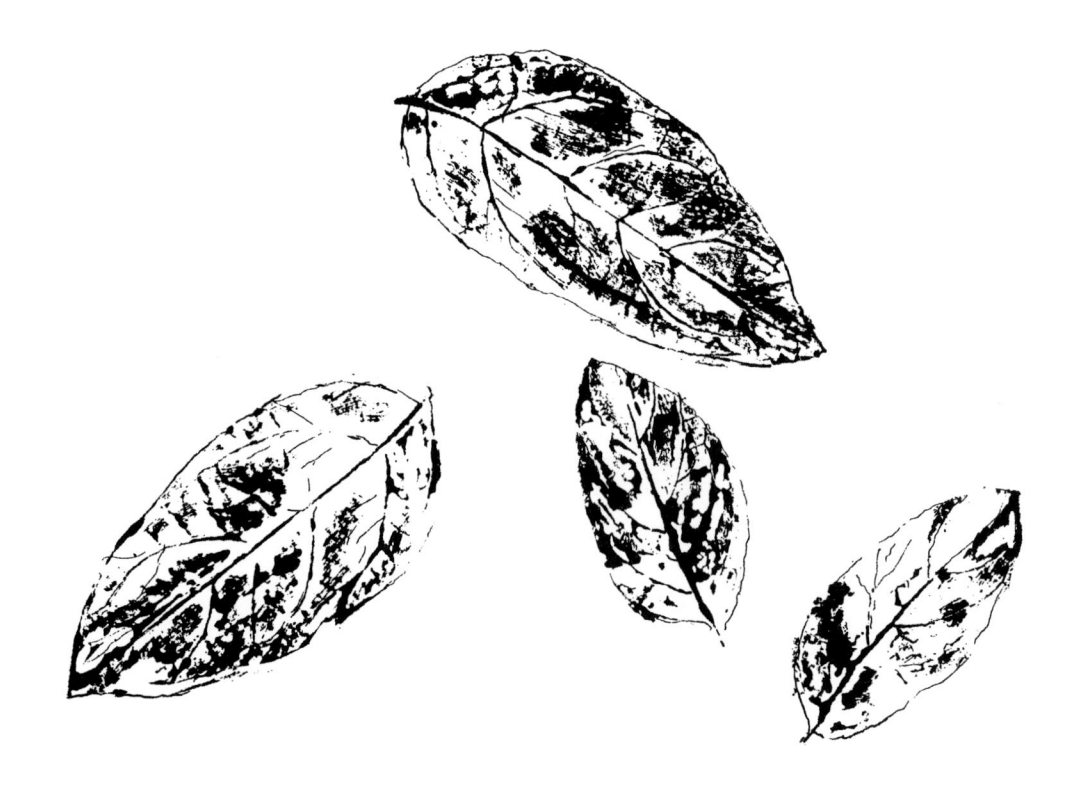

Blockprinting

Equipment and Materials

Small blocks of wood with felt shapes stuck on.
Ready mixed paint.
Large sheets of Paper.
Brushes.
Thick pads of felt.

Method

Squeeze small amount of paint onto pads.
Apply paint to blocks by pressing into pads.
Press blocks onto paper repeating prints several times.
If you wish to experiment further, make interesting prints with pieces of sponge, twists of material or paper etc.
As you will remember from school days, potatoes and other vegetables make good prints, as do fruits (especially lemons).

Fabric such as washed cotton can be block printed using thickened fabric dye, mixed with a binder (available from craft suppliers).

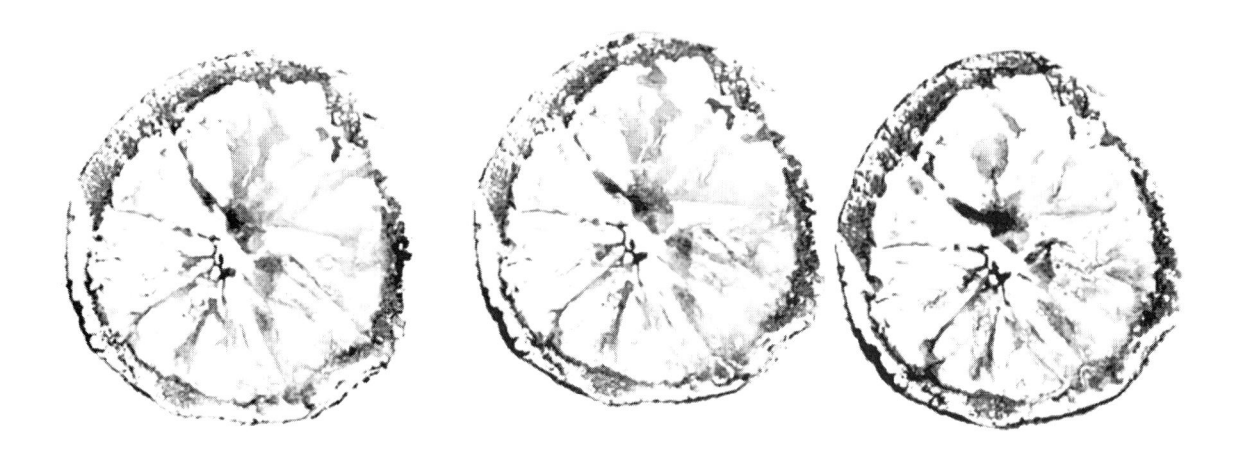

Decorating Paper - Stencilling

The American Colonists in the 18th century first used cut out designs in paper to decorate their homes, repeating the same motif to obtain an overall pattern.
Stencilling is an ideal method of producing greeting card designs for the elderly and the results are consistently good.
The brushes are dumpy and easy to hold, and a shaky hand doesn't matter.

Project - to produce a stencilled greeting card

Materials and Equipment

Poster paint or thick ready-mixed paint.
Stencil brushes.
Ready made stencils can be bought from craft suppliers or stencils can be made by cutting a design from manila paper, with a sharp craft knife. Treat with linseed oil.
Masking tape.
Kitchen paper.
Paper or card on which to produce design.

Method

Attach stencil to paper or card with masking tape.
Dip brush in paint and wipe away surplus paint on kitchen paper. The brush should be almost dry.
Hold brush in vertical position and stipple on the paint over design. A light mottled effect is very pleasing. Do not be too heavy.
Remove stencil.

As with all these craft ideas, the results will get better with practise.
A few embellishments with a gold pen gives a finishing touch.

When cutting your own designs, you may get away with using ordinary card instead of manila paper if you only want to use the stencil once.
The designs need to be distinctive and tend to work best when they are repeated to produce a border or overall pattern.
A very keen client may like to stencil onto a wooden box or piece of furniture.

Stencilled Christmas Cards

Christmas stencils can be bought from craft suppliers during November and December, to use with high quality coloured card. Another simple but effective way of producing a Christmas design is to stencil in reverse. Lay holly and ivy leaves onto card, and then gently spray with gold paint. Surprisingly, it does not seem to matter that the holly will not lay flat. The soft effect is very pleasing, but if you prefer a sharper holly shape, define the leaf outline with a gold, green or red pen. Small circles of red paper or felt can be stuck on to represent berries.

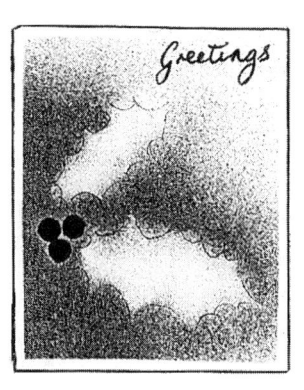

Project - Stencilled Stationery

An easy way of stencilling in reverse, on the bottom or top of notepaper

Materials And Equipment

Narrow strip of thin card approximately 5x21cm.
Pencil.
Scissors.
Paint i.e. thick ready mixed or poster paint.
Small dish.
Stencil brush or sponge.
Good quality plain paper A4 size.

Method

Fold card, concertina fashion.
Draw out a simple, connecting design and cut out.
Open out card and lay flat across top or bottom of paper
Dab a small amount of paint onto paper through holes in paper cutout, with sponge or brush.
Lift off and leave to dry.

You may decide to decorate the envelope in the same way.

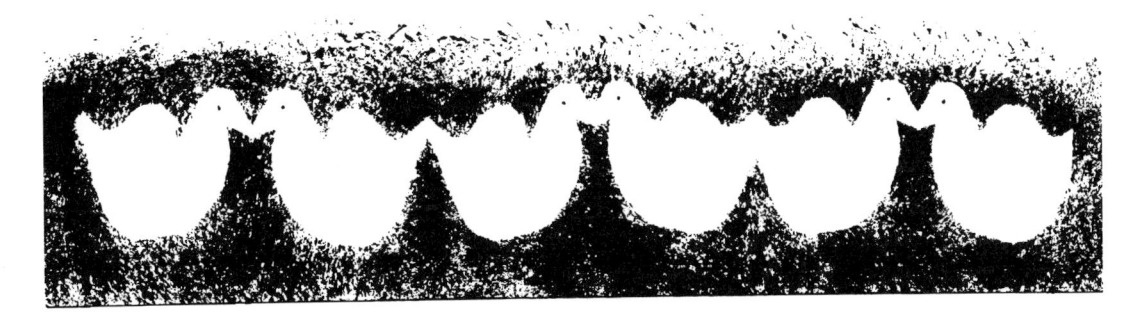

Gift Bags

Following on from sessions decorating paper, you may be looking for ideas to utilize the results. One suggestion follows, which is always popular as an item to make for a bazaar.

Project - Gift Bags

Materials And Equipment

A4 Paper.
Paper glue.
Scissors,
Ruler.
A hole punch.
Cord for the handles.

Method

Fold paper towards centre, overlapping by approximately 1cm. and crease folds.

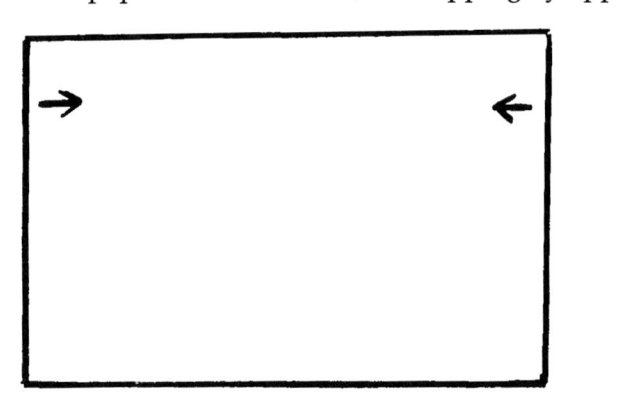

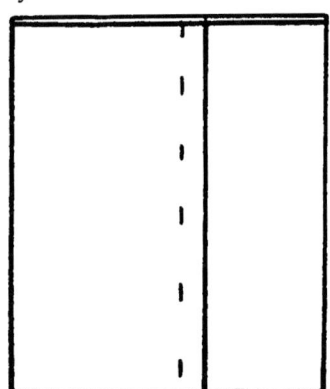

Glue seam and allow to dry. Fold up bottom 5cm, crease and fold.

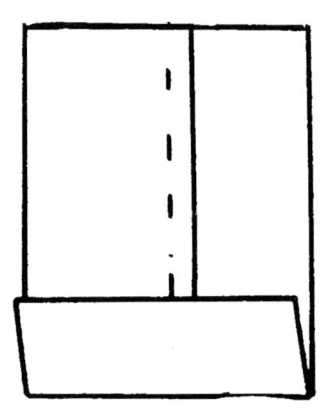

Unfold bottom section and push in sides of base.
Fold bottom flaps as diagrams, and crease.

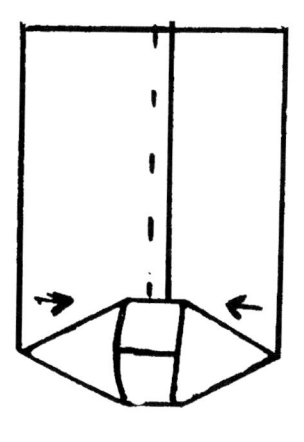

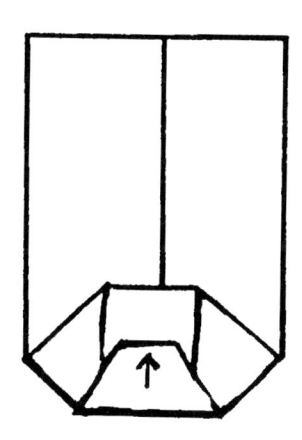

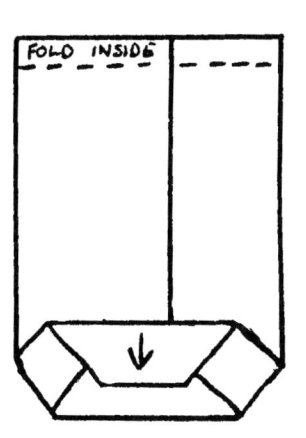

Open out folds, and glue.

Fold top edge down inside, approximately 5cm.
Punch holes in the top, threading through a length of cord to make handles.

If you run out of decorated paper, good quality gift wrap or wall paper samples can be used.

Why not make gift tags to match?

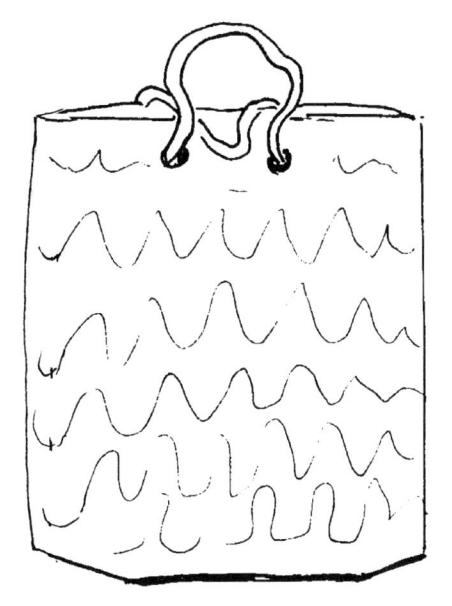

61

Chapter Four Arts and Crafts

Another Greeting Card Idea

A Teapot card to send to someone who lives a long way away.

Materials And Equipment

White or coloured card 25×32cm.
Tea bags.
Scissors and a stapler.
Access to a photocopier.
Decoration for front of card. e.g. a cut out from a used greeting card or magazine.

Method

Make template of teapot shape, and place on folded card.
Copy verse onto paper and paste inside (alternatively, copy directly onto card or best of all, if someone has decorative handwriting write the verse by hand)
Fold over and decorate front of card.
Staple tea bag inside.

If you wish to be more creative, a design can be painted or stencilled on the front of the teapot.

I'd like to come and visit you
And have a cup of tea.
But as you live so far away
Please have this one on me.

template

inside card

front

Papier-mâché

Down through the ages, papier-mâché has been used to make all kinds of decorative and useful objects, including furniture. A simple and inexpensive craft activity

Project - A papier-mâché Bowl

A bowl for fruit, sweets at Christmas-time or potpourri, depending on size.

Materials And Equipment

Newspaper.
Wallpaper paste (not containing fungicide).
Petroleum Jelly.
Coloured tissue paper.
Bowl to use as a mould.
Varnish (Paper varnish or polyurethane can be used but ventilation must be very good).
Small wallpaper brushes.
Scissors or craft knife.
Kitchen knife.

Method (Using Layering Technique).

Spread a layer of Petroleum Jelly inside or outside bowl.
Build up 8/10 layers of torn up (not cut) newspaper, pasting well with wallpaper paste.
Leave to dry between every 2/3 layers.
When complete and dry remove from mould with the kitchen knife.
Tidy around rim with scissors or craft knife.
Disguise sharp edge with a layer of pasted paper over the rim.
Apply a layer of torn white paper inside and outside the bowl to avoid news prints interfering with the decoration.
Allow to dry thoroughly.

Decoration

Build up layers of patches of coloured tissue paper, allow to dry,. and then varnish (This method is always successful in my experience).

Chapter Four Arts and Crafts

Decoupage

This craft, popular with the Victorians, is concerned with the process of decorating objects with cut out prints and then building up layers of varnish. This craft activity can naturally involve reminiscence.

Materials And Equipment

Something to decorate - e.g. a wooden box, card, flat picture frame,
Thin paper prints and illustrations from old magazines, wrapping paper etc. Greeting cards can be soaked and the backing paper peeled off. (This does not always work!)
Sharp scissors. Craft knives.
Sealer. Commercial sealer can be bought or made by mixing equal parts white spirit and varnish.
Soft brushes. Fine sandpaper.
Glue - usually wallpaper paste or P.V.A for wood.
Varnish - Polyurethane or preferably, a specialised varnish which dries quickly and fewer coats will be needed.

Method

Seal prints. Magazine prints should be sealed on both sides to prevent print showing through.
Cut out prints very carefully.
Plan design.
Apply adhesive and press down. Then allow to dry.
Apply as many coats of varnish as is necessary to achieve desired effect (up to 20 coats), sanding down between coats.

3-D Modern Decoupage

Another idea for Greeting Cards or a picture to frame

Materials And Equipment

At least four greeting cards of the same design. Boxes of Christmas cards are a good source, alternatively use good quality wrapping paper and folded plain card.
Small self-adhesive stickers.
Scissors.
Black felt tip pen.
Varnish.

Method

Use one card as a background.
Cut out sections of the main design from the remaining cards in a way that can achieve a raised up effect. For example;
If the card has an owl sitting on a snowy post, the owl and post could be cut out twice, the owls head and wings three times.
Any surrounding holly leaves could be cut out twice, with the occasional leaf cut out an extra time.
The cut edges can be touched with felt tip pen.
Apply the cut out sections with stickers, building up the 3 D effect.
Coat with spray varnish if desired.

Chapter Four Arts and Crafts

Preserving Flowers

Many garden flowers can be tied in bunches and hung up in a cool dry place.
Examples include: Helichrysum, Delphinium, Honesty, Hydrangea, Lavender, Statice and Love-in-a-Mist.
Grasses can be collected from the countryside.
Poppy heads are particularly prized for drying and using in summer and winter arrangements.
Dried flowers and grasses can be used for long lasting decorations in arrangements, and on greeting cards etc.

A herb ball will keep insects away and give aroma. Make by, pushing herbs e.g. rosemary, bay and mint into an Oasis ball.

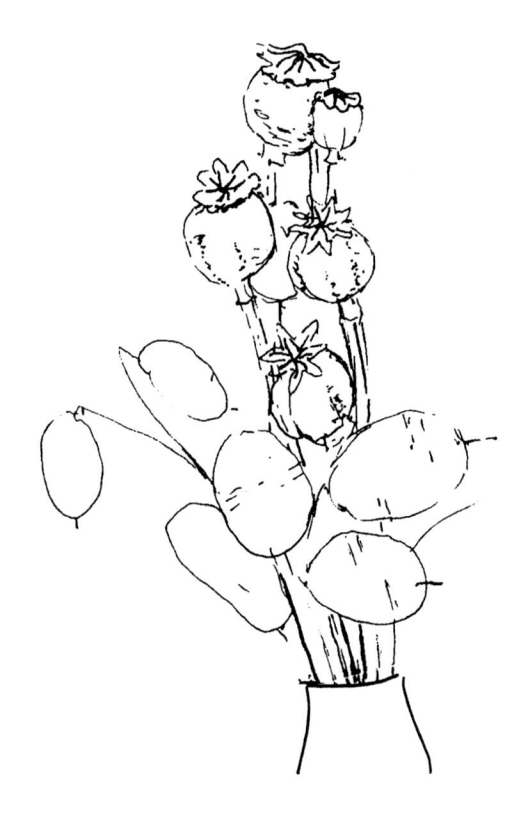

Poppy heads look good when sprayed gold at Christmas time. Honesty is useful in dried arrangements and when added to pressed flower pictures.

A straw hat can be decorated with dried flowers stuck on with Copydex.

Pressed Flowers

This is another craft that has connections with gardening, is familiar, and can have value in reminiscence sessions.

Suitable Flowers And Equipment

Simple flowers without a prominent seed area are best.
Delicate pictures can be made from garden flowers (Pansies work particularly well), or common wild flowers such as Buttercups and Daisies.
Leaves, grasses, and ferns will help the final composition.
Brightly coloured, Virginia Creeper leaves picked in the Autumn are very decorative.
Use secateurs and scissors for picking.
Use a flower press or heavy books and absorbent paper.

Points to remember

- Always pick in dry weather.
- Press as soon as possible.
- If using a book to press, weigh down well.
- Leave for approximately 6 weeks in a dry room.

Once pressed, use the flowers and leaves to decorate cards, candles, book marks etc.

Project - Decorate a Small Box

This is suitable for someone with a steady hand.

Materials And Equipment

Suitable box (available from craft suppliers or an old cigar box is ideal).
Pressed flowers.
Clear adhesive.
Spray varnish.
Tweezers.

Method

Pick up flowers with tweezers and add a touch of adhesive to the backs.
Position the flowers all over the box in an overlapping manner. Leave to dry.
Spray the whole box with varnish.

When spraying items like this box, stand the piece on a support and place it inside a large cardboard box, in a well ventilated area.

You may like to line the box with material.

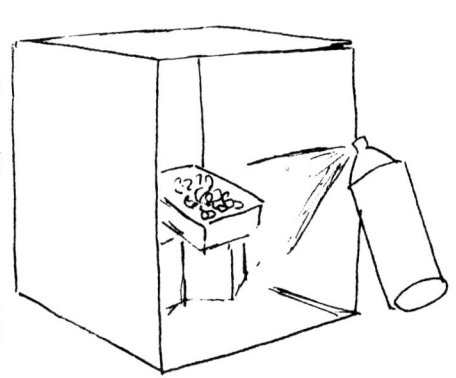

Chapter Four Arts and Crafts

Flower Arranging

We know from early paintings and engravings, that the pleasures of arranging cut flowers and greenery date back to early times.

Most of the elderly lady clients and many of the staff, will have tried this craft. This can be an inexpensive hobby as fresh flowers, greenery, grasses, and interesting pieces of twig can usually be found at all seasons of the year. Most homes and centres have a garden where flowers could be grown for drying to be used in arrangements. Even in the depth of winter there are brightly coloured berries to make up for the scarcity in flowers.

Materials

Oasis - easily available from garden centres and florists, but remember to buy grey for dried flowers and green for fresh flowers.

There are lots of other ways of supporting the flowers, but Oasis is the most suitable for elderly people in my experience. However, you could provide stub wires, chicken wire or anything else that you like.

Containers - small purpose made ones into which the Oasis fits well can be bought very cheaply from florists.

Green tape can also be bought to secure the Oasis.

Scissors and secateurs.

Flowers, greenery, berries etc.

Method

Once the Oasis has been secured, and soaked if necessary, everyone can be encouraged to produce their own design.

The clients should make their own choices of colour, shape etc.

The arrangements work best when they are kept smallish for the first attempts with sufficient small pieces to use low down in order to hide the Oasis.

At Christmas time, of course you can use holly, spruce, and ivy.
Add a bright red candle and you have a table centre.

Encourage conversation to develop, whilst listening to the clients views and tips from the past.

Perhaps if everyone is keen, someone from the local Flower Arranging Club would like to give a demonstration.

68

Potpourri

During the sixteenth century, English homes were sometimes built with a Still Room, where sweet smelling herbs and flowers were hung to dry and mixed into potpourri. In fact, references to potpourri can be found in the records of many ancient cultures including the ancient Greeks. Today, potpourri can be bought from shops, but the process of collecting and drying fragrant flowers is not complicated, and is particularly appreciated by elderly people, as it relates to gardening and the countryside.
Very dependant clients who are unable to physically participate will enjoy the fragrance.

Ingredients

Fragrant plants and flowers.
Fixatives(e.g. Orrisroot Powder - available from old fashioned chemists).
Essential Oils-a quick way to add to fragrance or refresh potpourri.

Method

Dry by spreading flowers on absorbent paper and turning at regular intervals over several days/weeks.
Once dry, place the dried flower mixture in a paper bag and sprinkle liberally with fixative.
Shake regularly for about four weeks.
Add a few drops of appropriate oil if, necessary, in order to increase perfume.
Use as required.

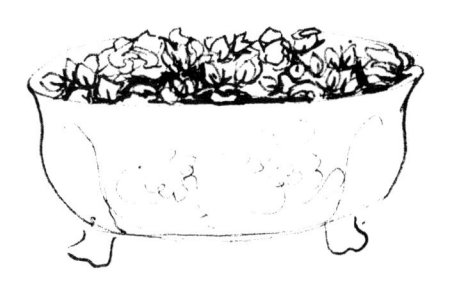

Paper Flowers

Making paper flowers is always popular, because with a little help, everyone will end up with a flower of sorts. If it does not quite turn out as intended, never mind, it can be called a peony or daffodil, whatever it resembles most!.

The flowers can all be put together to decorate the table, to put individually into specimen vases or as one group that I worked with did, to decorate Easter Bonnets.

Project - Crepe Paper Roses

This project will stimulate memories as clients recall the roses being made by Romany Gypsies years ago, who used to fix them on a privet twig and sell them along with the pegs.

Materials and Equipment

Coloured crepe paper
Scissors
Florist Stub Wires
Reel of thin wire
Blunt knife

Method

Cut a strip of crepe paper across the grain. Size and length depends on the size of flower required, but 10cm by 1 metre is a start.
Cut a scallop shape (5cm. approximately), along the long edge.
(Cut this folded if you wish.)

Stretch each scallop gently between knife and thumb to produce petals
Gradually roll the length of scalloped paper up, gathering as you go. Make sure that the petals curl outwards.
Cut out a small level section in the middle to make a centre.
Secure the flower with a florist wire, which can also provide a stem.
Cut a leaf shape and secure to stem with thin wire.
A thin strip of green crepe paper (cut across the grain), can be wrapped around (stretching slightly) to hide the wire.

Knitting

Any needlecraft is usually easy for elderly ladies to relate to, as it has so often been a part of everyday life. A regular 'Knit and Natter' afternoon, provides a time for a member of staff to bring interested clients together to exchange patterns, admire work and possibly work on a joint project. Everyone can happily work whilst chatting to friends. The experienced knitter can help the inexperienced.
Large print patterns, thick wool, row counters and large needles are all easily available.
There is no reason why someone who has not knitted before should not learn, with some help and encouragement. There will almost certainly be a client or member of staff who can knit, and so could teach a newcomer this craft.

Here is the simplest of knitting patterns.

Project - A Knitted Dishcloth.

Materials And Equipment

A ball of dish cloth cotton.
Size 5-7mm. needles.

Method

Cast on sufficient stitches to make a 25cm. square.
Work in garter stitch (just plain), until the bottom right hand corner can reach the top left hand corner.
Keep work loose.
Cast off.

Rugs

Rugs can be woven, hooked, plaited, knitted or crocheted. Any method could be used for a group projec to be brought out from time to time.

Project - A Traditional Rag Rug

This project is ideal as a group craft activity, and as a means to stimulate memories. Long winter evenings, in the past, were often taken up by the ladies in the family cutting up cast off clothing, to make into rugs.

Materials

A piece of hessian, traditionally a washed sack opened out. Shops selling wild bird food may be able to supply a hessian sack, or you may be able to beg one from a friendly farmer.
Washed woollen coat, skirts etc.
Hook (traditionally a specially adapted wooden peg).
Scissors.

Method

Cut long strips of material, traditionally cut in a spiral between the seams so as to waste as little as possible. You should end up with a long strip which can be wound into a ball.
The long strip is hooked through the hessian into lots of loops, making a pattern with areas of different colour.
Half of the opened out sack is covered with the hooked strips and the other half is folded under to make a backing, oversewn all the way round. A piece of blanket can be inserted at this stage.

This method was shown to me by a group of elderly ladies at a day hospital in the Forest of Dean. The more widely used method involves using lots of short lengths (about 10cm) hooking through the hessian once, or knotting like a latchhooked rug.

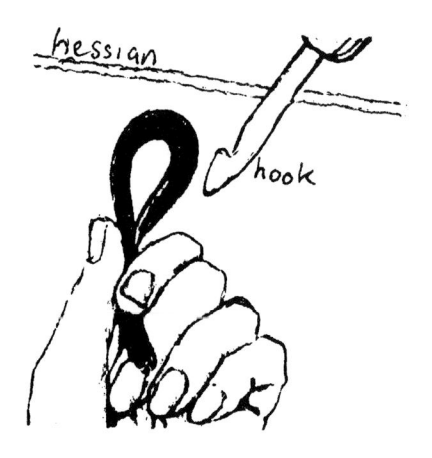

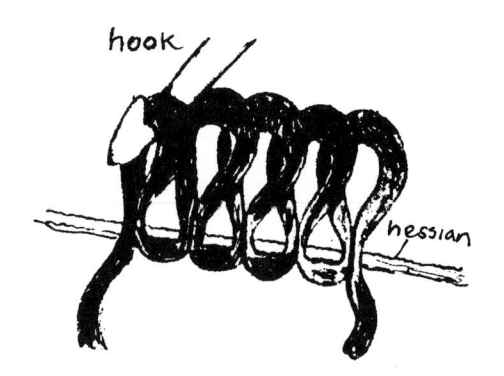

Chapter Four Arts and Crafts

Project - a Latch Hooked Rug

Materials and Equipment

A length of rug canvas (ready - painted, or paint your own design on with acrylic paint).
Ready - cut rug wool.
Latch Hooks (several, so that two or three people can work together)

Method

When people are working from opposite ends, both knot methods will have to be used, to ensure that the pile will lie in the same direction.

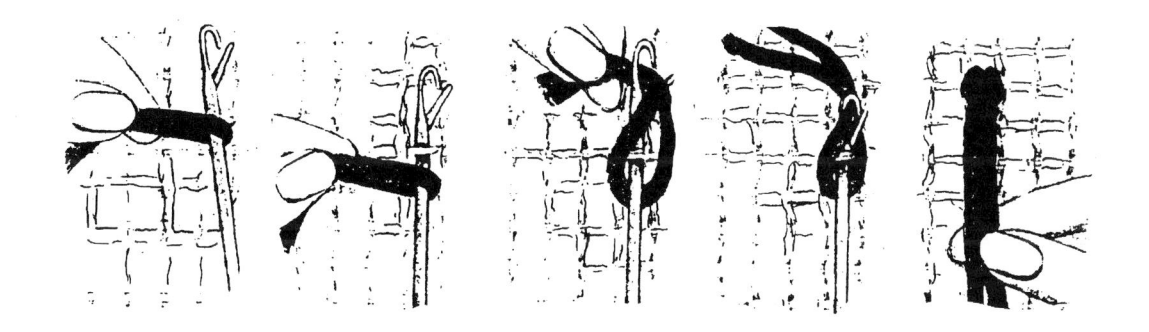

method one

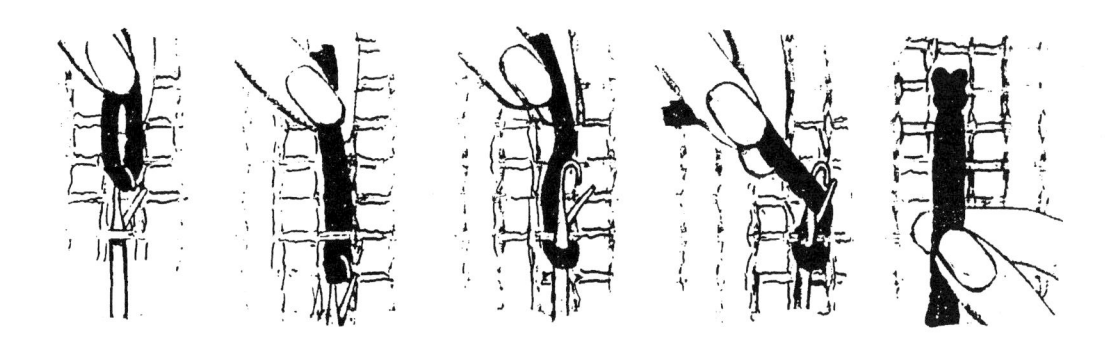

method two

73

Patchwork

In the past, patchwork was born out of necessity. The best scraps of material were saved from worn garments and sewn together to produce bedcovers, cushion covers etc. Over the years complicated patterns developed, in order to make the end product more decorative, and the process more interesting.

Project - A very simple handsewn quilt

The quilt can be made to any size from pram size to bed size, depending on the number of squares produced. As patchwork is made up of individual simple components it is always a successful group activity, with everyone working within their capabilities. At one day centre where I work the craft group regularly made a pram quilt for pregnant members of staff going on maternity leave.

Materials and Equipment

100% cotton scraps of material (washed).
Thin card from which to make templates. (Old Greeting Cards are the correct thickness).
Scissors.
Ruler.
Pencil.
Needle and Cotton.

Method

Cut 2 inch and 4 inch squares from card, accurately, to make the templates.
Cut 3 inch and 5 inch squares from the material to allow for seam allowances. Try to choose colours that will compliment one another, or so many different colours and patterns that the overall effect will look good.
Place the templates on the material squares.

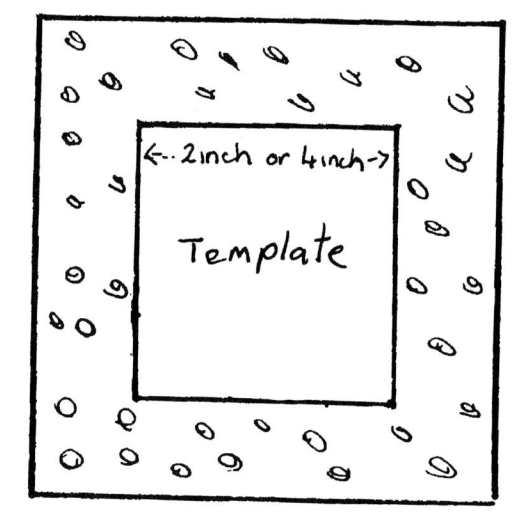

Fold seam allowance over the edge of the card templates and tack. Either push the needle through the card or not as you wish, but it will be easier to remove the templates if you have not tacked through the card. (Clients with dexterity problems may find the larger squares easier to handle)

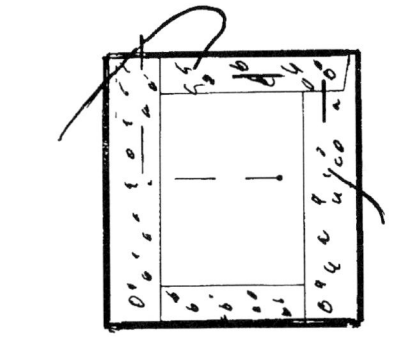

Once enough patches have been tacked by the group, they can be laid out in an agreed design.

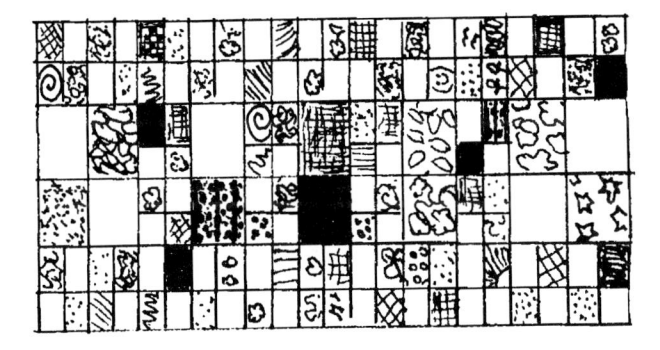

The patches are then oversewn together, facing patches right sides together.

To finish off, the card templates and tacking is removed.
The patchwork can then be pressed and backed with a suitably sized length of cotton backing. A filling of wadding or a washable blanket will add weight and warmth.

75

Cross Stitch

Cross Stitch is a suitable choice for most elderly clients to have a go at. There is just the one basic stitch and the fabric of choice, Aida, comes in a wide variety of mesh sizes, to cater for everyone's visual capability. Magnifying lenses manufactured for the needleworker can be bought from Craft Suppliers.

The basic stitch is very simple. Just make sure that the top diagonal stitch is always slanting in the same direction. For the first smallish attempt a frame will not be needed. If the client is keen to try larger more complicated designs, then a frame will be a necessary investment, to ensure that the fabric keeps it's shape.
A very reasonably priced frame for a client who only has the use of one hand, is available from T.F.H. (ref. Contacts page)

Materials and Equipment

All easily available from craft shops.
Fabric (Aida).
Silks.
Blunt ended tapestry needles.
Scissors.
Frame.

Designs

Ready printed designs can be bought.
Photographs can be transferred onto the fabric using a colour photocopier.
Designs can be transferred from a chart by counting the squares.
After a first experimentation a client may like to produce an original design on graph paper and transfer by counting.

A simple geometric design can be used for the first attempt, using two colours. The pattern can be counted on the Aida with a felt tip pen.

Chapter Four Arts and Crafts

Crochet

Crochet designs are built up on a series of chain stitches, using a hook and yarn. Crochet enthusiasts tend to develop their own way of starting work with the yarn.

Method

An easy way to start.

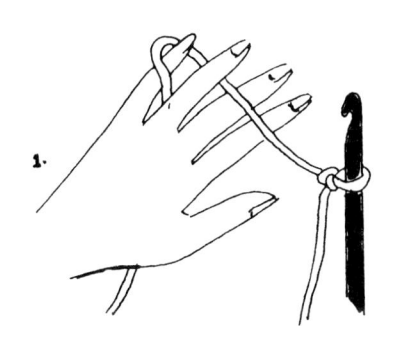

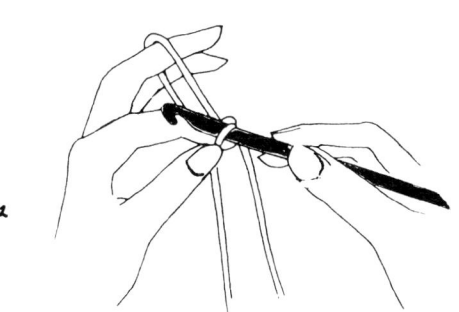

❶Taking up the yarn.   ❷Hands in position.   ❸Chain stitch

Double Crochet is the most widely used basic stitch. As a project, a client may like to trim a blanket or garment.
Using the chain as a foundation :
❶Hook under 2nd chain. ❷Catch yarn with hook. ❸Draw loop through, which gives 2 loops on hook. ❹Catch yarn again and draw through both loops on hook.

Repeat this action into every chain loop to the end and you will have completed a row of double crochet.

Easy-to-do and large print patterns are available for clients wishing to develop the skills of Crochet or Knitting.

Health and Safety Hints for Craft Sessions

- Good ventilation is necessary when using solvents, oil based paints, melting wax etc.

- All tools to be kept in good condition, and accounted for at the end of each session.

- Use protective gloves and clothing as appropriate.

- Be aware of smoking rules, and Fire Drill, and location of First Aid Box..

- Have a list of emergency phone numbers available

- A calm, well ordered, environment helps to avoid accidents

- The size of the group should be limited to a number that can be supervised.

- Watch each client use tools before allowing your attention to go elsewhere.

Home Crafts

Cooking Sessions in a Nursing Home Setting

Sights, sounds and smells from the kitchen, bring back so many memories for elderly ladies, who spent so much of their life cooking for a family. This is an opportunity for us to learn from our clients.

Suggestions

- Compile a written collection of recipes and cooking tips. Could some of the recipes be tried out by the clients or the cook?
- Organise a session looking at traditional recipes, cookery books, and old advertisements. This will lead to discussion about the changes in methods over the years.
- One or two clients may like to accompany a member of staff into the kitchen to bake a cake or make marmalade.
- Organise a fun session with a member of staff cooking pancakes in the Day Room on a hot plate, so that everyone can watch and enjoy eating the results.
- Organise a productive session producing homemade sweets or petit fours, to sell at a coffee morning.
- Collect empty small Baked Bean tins. Make a fruit cake mixture, using the tins to cook small, individual cakes, so that everyone in the group can ice and decorate to their own design.
- A resident or a member of staff from a differing ethnic background, may like to talk about, or demonstrate their traditional cooking.
- If a resident has a special friend or relative coming to visit, he or she may like to bake a cake, to demonstrate continued independence.

Gardening

> *"If you want to be happy for an hour, get drunk*
> *If you want to be happy for a year, get married*
> *If you want to be happy for ever, get a garden"*
> Chinese Proverb

Tending plants and watching them grow, does seem to have a healing effect and is an ongoing source of pleasure throughout many peoples lives. It also brings people out into the fresh air, so we should provide a safe pathway into and around the garden. Specially planned gardens and modified tools, can enable older people with disabilities to continue with their hobby for as long as possible.
Residents in most homes have been encouraged to bring in items of furniture when they moved in. Could they transplant a few plants from their garden?

The progress of tomato growth seems to be a regular topic of conversation during the summer months at day centres that are lucky enough to have a greenhouse.
For nursing home clients, to have access to a greenhouse in which to grow plants or bring on seedlings, gives a sense of control over ones environment and the chance to retain a hobby.

Without a greenhouse, the opportunities for gardening are still many, especially with help and encouragement from members of staff. The clients are then able to pass on the knowledge gained from their past experience.

By nurturing a wild area in the garden, we can attract butterflies and give a reminder of the countryside to the clients who may not be able to go out very often. Herbs and other sweet smelling plants, moving water, and wind chimes can be enjoyed by partially sighted clients.

More Suggestions

- Spring bulbs can be planted in bowls.
- Hanging Baskets can be planted.
- Pips and seeds can be collected to produce house plants.
- A tomato or cucumber plant can be grown on a sunny window sill.
- House plants can be tended and propagated.
- Compile a collection of gardening tips.
- Make a regular event of the group watching a television gardening programme and encourage discussion afterwards.
- Arrange picnics and barbecues to encourage clients into the garden.

Bouquet Garni Sachets

Clients may like to pick parsley, thyme and bay leaves and make Bouquet Garni sachets for use in the kitchen. The sachets are made by drying and packing into small sachets sewn from washed muslin. Keep sachets in an air tight container.

Chapter Five Outings, Events and Entertainment

Rationale

An outing organised from a club or day centre, is an opportunity for isolated people to get out and about, in the company of others.

An outing from a nursing home is an opportunity for people who may have little contact with the outside world, to go out whilst in the company of friends, whom they can trust.

Events and entertainment can be of enormous benefit in adding spice and interest to life. If the clients have been involved in the planning, and encouraged to contribute as much as possible to the event, feelings of self worth are given a boost.

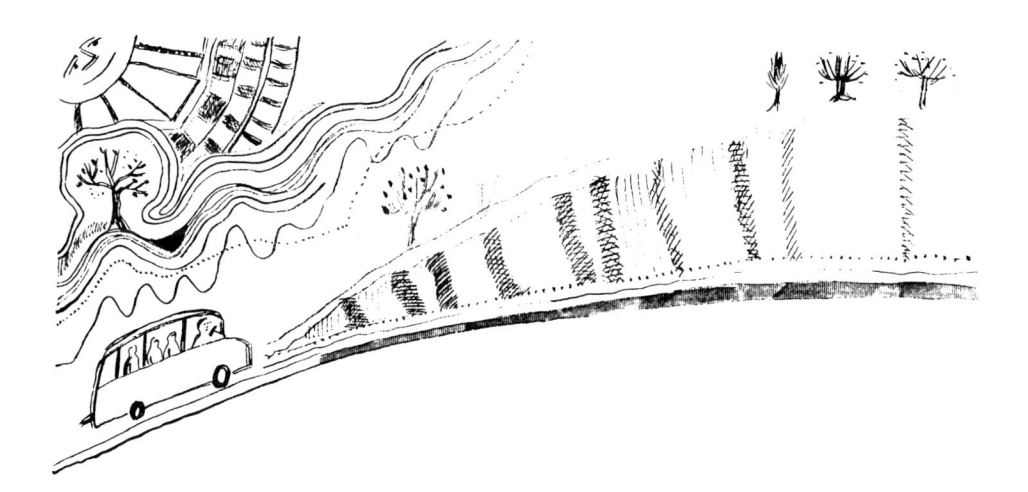

Outings

It is by no means easy to decide which events will be well supported even with full client consultation. In my experience it is a common situation that, a large number of clients will sometimes 'put their name down' for a particular outing and most of them will change their mind on the day. Whilst we do not wish to resort to coercion, we find ourselves putting a certain amount of pressure on the client, as so often, clients say in retrospect that they had a good time and were glad that they had been persuaded to go. Once again, we have to know how far we can go in our encouragement. From the clients point of view, he or she may feel safer in his or her daily routine, and be apprehensive about the physical effort involved in the preparation.

Forward Planning

A group outing with very dependant clients will need one to one staff support.
Buses should be adapted to take wheelchairs.
Medication, medical equipment, food including special diets must be organized.
There is a great deal of research to be done into the availability of toilets, the negotiability of hills, etc.
After a great deal of planning, everyone can relax, have a great deal of fun and have lots to laugh and talk about when they come home. Don't forget the camera !

Venue Suggestions For Day Trips

Countryside picnics.
Visits to places of interest.
Shopping trips.
Visits to cinemas, theatre.
Visits to the seaside.
Local events, fêtes and flower shows.
Boat trips.
Going to a pub for a bar snack.
Visiting a show farm.
A trip out to look at the autumn colours.
Heritage Centres, Folk Museums and other places of interest.
Bird Sanctuaries (such as at Slimbridge, Gloucestershire, which has level pathways)
School Concerts.
Botanical gardens.
An Airport.

Events and Entertainment

This heading can cover so much. Here are some more tried and tested ideas for you to suggest to your clients.

A Sports Day

Hopefully apart from having fun and fund raising from sponsors, this event will encourage team spirit and a sense of achievement.
Whilst we could not aim for a decathlon, we could include a tiddlywinks championship, darts, dominoes, skittles, and a sponsored stroll around the garden for more active clients and a staff sponsored walk!

A Slide Show

This type of event promotes a group feeling and is great fun.
Apart from the usefulness for reminiscence sessions, a showing of slides of local beauty spots always goes down well.
As there was a craze for taking slides in the 1960's and 70's there should be one or two members of staff with sides tucked away in their attics. These images of their now grown up families dressed in 60's and 70's fashions will be fascinating to the group.
Serve refreshments and possibly invite visitors to increase the sense of occasion.

Does The Centre Or Home Own A Video Player?

A Video Club can encourage independence and awareness of other peoples needs.
Clients can take turns to hire a video after consulting the group. Visit the shop if possible.
Make an evenings entertainment with the viewing of the video and refreshments half way through.

Organise a Speaker

The local library or information centre should be able to supply a list of contact telephone numbers for groups, who may be able to supply a speaker.
Suggestions for possible speakers could be; a gardening expert, a craft worker, a health worker, or a local author.
You should confirm details in writing, such as time and date, and what the expenses or fee will be.
Encourage the client group to consider in advance, what questions might be interesting. The group might like to organise one of the members to say a welcoming few words, and a thank you.

Organise a Concert

Once again, the local library should be able to help. Local groups such as : a choir, town band, bell ringers, local school, could be approached to provide a concert. The Council for Music in Hospitals (refer to contact list) arranges concerts by professional musicians in hospitals, homes and centres, with elderly people in mind.

Chapter Five Outings, Events and Entertainment

The provision of the large room with easy access for wheelchairs should not present a problem, but the performers may need somewhere to use as a dressing room.. Involve the clients in planning the event at all stages. Some of the expenses involved could be recovered by inviting friends and families and selling refreshments and raffle tickets.

Play Reading

Many elderly people were involved in amateur dramatics. Ask at your library for suitable plays.

A Photograph Gallery

This event has potential for reminiscence, helps people to get to know one another and results in lots of laughter.
Ask all staff and clients to bring in photographs of themselves as babies or young children. Pass them all round for everyone to look at, which will take much longer than you would expect.
Pin the photographs up for a 'guess who this is' competition.
Staff, clients and visitors will be fascinated and this is good for fund raising.

Obtain an up to date photographs of each member of staff (not posed, at work or home) with name and post written underneath, and pin them up in the foyer of the Centre or Home. This will be a talking point and invaluable for visitors.
The presentation of the up to date photographs could be a craft activity.

Suggestions

A card frame could be made for each photograph.
A collage design could be produced and the photographs stuck on.
e.g. a tree with photographs on the leaves or a garden with a staff member looking out from each flower.

Guess Where This Is?

Photographs of unusual angles around the Home or Centre are passed around and pinned up for everyone to puzzle over: e.g. An aerial view from a ladder, from outside a window looking in, or inside a cupboard etc. etc.

Bingo

This game gives so much pleasure and seems to be part of some peoples culture.
For the partially - sighted clients, enlarge the bingo cards on a photocopier.
Braille numbers can be obtained from the R.N.I.B. The hard of hearing can sit near the front, and have hearing aids insitu and turned on. Don't forget to say;

On its own number one.
Kelly's eye number one.
Legs eleven number eleven.
Key of the door twenty one.
Clickerty click sixty six.

Two fat ladies eighty eight.
All the threes thirty three etc.
Downing Street number ten.
Unlucky for some thirteen.
Droopy draws forty four.

Chapter Six Seasonal Activities and Theme Days

Rationale

Bring cohesion to a range of activities by sticking to a definite theme. This tends to happen naturally at the special holiday times like Christmas, Easter, Harvest Festival etc., resulting in memories of past family occasions

There are endless possibilities for theme days and they provide an opportunity to cover the full range of activities. Choosing a country for a theme is particularly helpful where clients or staff are from varying ethnic backgrounds.

All the senses can be simulated as craft sessions, entertainment, word games, decorations and mealtimes all reflect the theme.

Christmas Projects

Wrapping Presents

Encourage group activity, communication, reminiscence, and have fun, by gathering all interested clients together, to make their presents look extra special.

Simple Ideas for home made Wrapping Paper

Materials And Equipment

Plain Paper e.g. Lining paper, Sugar Paper.
Embossed Wallpaper.
Chalk.
Ready Mixed Paint.
Shallow Containers for paint.
Scissors.
Double sided tape.
Pieces of Sponge.
Potatoes.
Ribbon etc.

Methods

Block Prints see page 57.

Designing a Pattern with a sponge i.e.:
Dip sponge in paint and dab over paper.
Wash sponge and repeat with harmonising colour.
Make tag to match.

Using Embossed Wallpaper :
Wrap present (box shape).
Use double sided tape to secure.
Rub wax crayons or chalk over surface, highlighting motifs.
Remove loose chalk with a tissue.

Adding the Finishing Touch

Parcels can be finished off with lots of ribbon curling the ends with a blunt knife. Florists ribbon is very inexpensive and curls very well.
Paper or dried flowers can be added.
Christmas shapes such as bells holly or Christmas trees can be cut from foil and stuck on. Add glitter. Christmas card suggestions see page 59.

A Christmas Pomander

Pomanders were originally made to hang from belts to protect the wearer from foul smells and infection.
When made in early December and hung up at Christmas time they make an attractive and sweet smelling decoration.

Materials And Equipment

An Orange.
Whole cloves.
Cinnamon.
Orris root powder (available from an old fashioned chemist).
Red ribbon.

Method

Press cloves all over orange in rows (a thimble comes in useful), leaving room to place ribbon.
Brush with cinnamon and orrisroot powder.
Wrap in grease proof paper and store in a drawer until Christmas.
Loop ribbon around pomander to hang up.

Simple Christmas decoration ideas

Tree decorations can be made from salt dough (see page 53).
Christmas pastry cutters can be used if available, to make bells, trees and angels and then painted.
Candle rings can also be made from salt dough decorated with dough pieces in the shape of holly leaves.
Paint with acrylic paint.

Collect large seed pods, cones, nuts and berries.
Spray them gold and arrange in a bowl

Slice oranges and lemons and dry in an airing cupboard for several days, turning from time to time.
Tie up the slices adding cinnamon sticks, with red ribbon to wreaths and other greenery.

Use bright and shiny 'twist end' wrapped sweets to make a tree decoration.
Punch a hole in the twist end and thread through a ribbon or bead chain. (Remember to provide some diabetic sweets).

Make Golden Angels for the Tree

Materials and Equipment

Gold backed paper.
Polystyrene balls for head.
Trimmings.
Strong glue.
Florist wire.
Scissors.

Method

Concertina two rectangles of paper, one larger than the other.
Gather the end together of the larger one and glue.
Pinch together the centre of the smaller one and glue.
Fix together to form a skirt and wings with glue. Reinforce with staples if necessary.
Fix head on top with wire
Decorate with wool for hair
Cover joins with gold ribbon.

Fabric Tree Decorations.

Materials And Equipment

Material scraps.
Padding.
Templates in the shape of hearts, circles, bells etc.
Needle and cotton, scissors, thimble.
Trimmings, ribbons, Sequins.

Method

Cut two shapes from bright material scraps.
Sew around the shapes and pad.
Decorate with sequins.
Hang up with a paper clip or ribbon

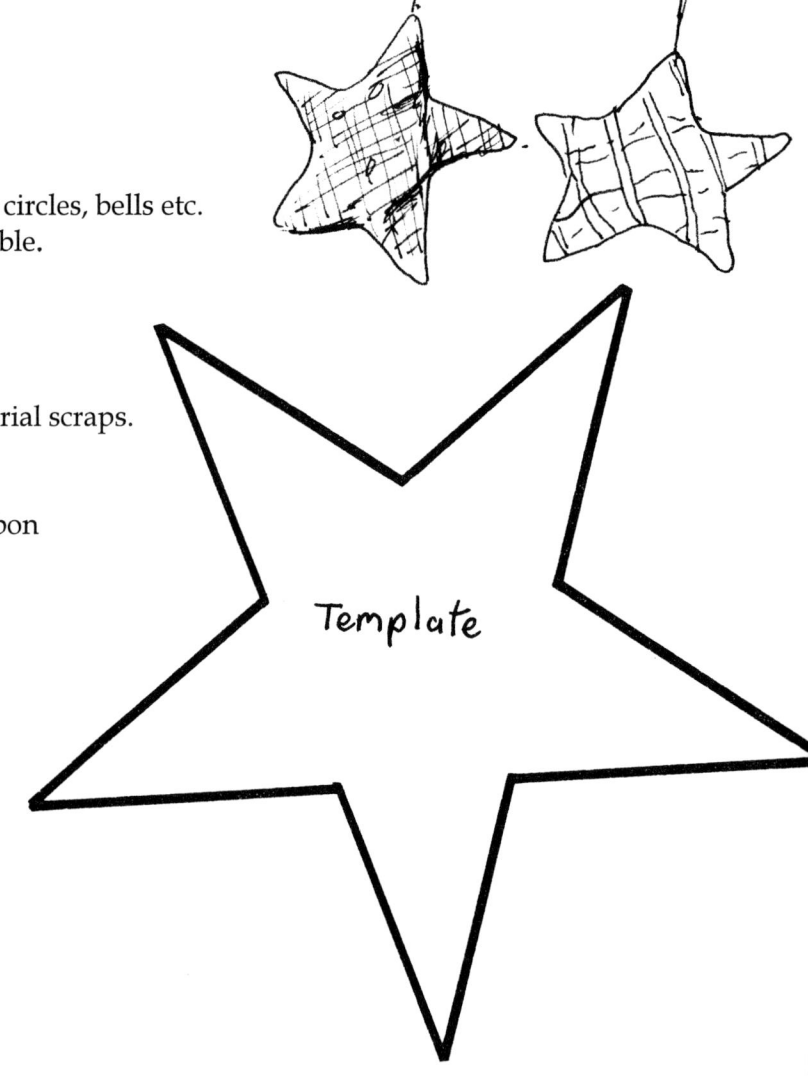

Template

Stimulate All The Senses

Guess The Christmas Smell

Fill opaque, lidded containers with typical seasonal smells -
i.e. spices, orange, pine leaves, wine, chocolate.
Make holes in the lids and pass the containers round for everyone to guess the smell.

A Christmas Sound Quiz

Record a selection of sounds associated with the season, some easy and some difficult -
e.g. church bells, mixing a cake, pouring wine, opening parcels,
a crackling log fire, carol singers, a few words from the Queens speech, etc.

A Christmas Music Quiz

Record snippets from well known Christmas songs and carols, so that the group can sit together and guess the tune. Finish up with a sing-song.

A Christmas Quiz

Bring everyone together in a group, so that everyone can hear, and make sure that there is a variety of questions so that no-one is left out.
Here are some questions to start you off.

- Q. Who had a red nose in the Christmas song?
- A. Rudolf.

- Q. What did the three kings bring to the stable?
- A. Gold, Frankincense and Myrrh.

- Q. How does snow form?
- A. Frozen droplets of water form crystals, no two of which are the same.

- Q. What country presents a Christmas tree to London each year?
- A. Norway.

- Q. From which carol do the words, 'Deep and crisp and even' come from?
- A. Good King Wensleslas
  Can you sing it?

- Q. What do we call a tree that does not lose its leaves in winter?
- A. Evergreen.

- Q. Can you name any animals that hibernate for the winter months?
- A. Hedgehog, Squirrel.

- Q. Can you name any Christmas time flowers?
- A. Pointsettia, Christmas Rose, Winter Jasmin.

- Q. Name Dickens characters associated with Christmas.

Chapter Six Seasonal Activities and Theme Days

A. Scrooge, Tiny Tim.

Q. Which Christmas song, in which film did Bing Crosby make famous?
A. 'White Christmas' in 'Holiday Inn'.
Can you sing it?

Q. For how long would you cook a 2lb Christmas pudding for, in advance and on the day?
A. 6 hours and 2 hours(I think!).

Q. During which reign was the Christmas message to the commonwealth first recorded?
A. George V.

Q. How does a Scotsman first foot?
A. Calling on friends and neighbours, bringing in coal and whisky after midnight on New Years Eve.

Q. List as many Christmas foods as you can.

Q. What was the huge log called that was burnt as fuel at Christmas time?
A Yule Log.

Q. Why is mincemeat so called?
A. It used to contain meat.

Q. What was hidden in puddings at Christmas?
A. A tiny silver threepenny bit.

Q. Why is the 21st. December significant?
A. It is known as the solstice, when daylight is at its least.

Q. In what town was the stable where Christ was born.
A. Bethlehem.

Q. Can you name what was sent on each day of Christmas in the famous Christmas song?
A. Twelve drummers, eleven pipers, ten lords, nine ladies, eight maids, seven swans, six geese, five gold rings, four calling birds, three french hens, two turtle doves and a partridge in a pear tree!
Can you sing it?

Q. Can anyone in the group tell of any Christmas or midwinter customs from other cultures?

Q. What are similar characters to Father Christmas called in other parts of the world?
A. Santa Claus; Saint Nicholas.

90

Easter Projects

An Easter Bonnet Parade is traditional and a great deal of fun for those that want to join in. Old hats can be decorated with paper flowers, feathers etc.
Hot Cross Buns can be handed round with the refreshments.

Make spring flower arrangements to decorate the home or centre.

Chocolate moulds can be bought and used to make Eggs and Rabbits
Cooking chocolate can be bought in bulk and melted down by the clients. The results can then be sold to help funds.

Ask the group to share customs and memories relating to Easter and Springtime.

Arrange an hour of Easter hymns and songs.

Easter is very important on the Christian calendar, and it is also a special time for other faiths and cultures. Can any client or member of staff talk about less familiar spring celebrations?

Egg Decorating

At Easter time, we will probably be hunting for some seasonal ideas for an activity session. Egg decorating comes to mind, but it is important not to make the session seem childish. These ways of decorating the eggs is more unusual and the results could be used for an Easter Fayre.

Preparing the Eggs

The easiest way of preparing the eggs is to hard boil them for at least half an hour. They will then last indefinitely.

Egg Decorating- Using cold water dye

Scratch a pattern into the hard boiled egg. Dye the egg a rich dark colour. The scratched pattern will be beautifully defined.

Dip tiny fern leaves in olive oil and arrange around hard boiled egg. Dab off excess oil with tissue. Keep leaves in place using a section of an old pair of tights. Soak eggs in the dye until the correct shade is achieved and remove fern leaves and tights. You should be left with a beautifully patterned egg.

Use the dyes (easily obtainable from shops and craft suppliers) as if you were dyeing fabric.

Egg Decorating- Using Natural Vegetable Dyes

Yellow - Use onion and saffron - Rather expensive
Brown - Use onion skin and coffee.
Red - Use Onion skin, beetroot juice and and vinegar.
Green - Use spinach.

Boil the eggs with the vegetable, until it is the shade that you require.

More Egg Decorating Ideas

Cut tiny shapes from coloured tissue paper. Stick onto hard boiled egg (which could have been previously dyed), with white P.V.A glue. Add another coat of glue to give a glossy surface, or a coat of pearl nail polish can look good.

Stick on small dried leaves and flower petals with clear nail polish. Add a final coat of varnish.

Trail on melted wax with a batik tool before soaking in cold water dye.

Paint on designs with acrylic paint.

Harvest Festival

All around the world people have celebrated the bringing in of the harvest. The ancient Greeks feasted in honour of the harvest goddess, the Chinese celebrate Harvest Moon and in America, Thanksgiving, on the last Thursday in November, is a national holiday.

Ask the group if they would like to decorate the room for a Harvest Festival.

Make a Large Mural using coloured leaves, nuts, twigs etc. Leave a space in the middle, so that it can be used as large poster advertising the Harvest Events.

Organise a session reading Autumn Poems.
This famous poem is by John Keats

To Autumn

Season of mists and mellow fruitfulness,
Close bosom friend of the maturing sun,
Conspiring with him how to load and bless
With fruit the vines that round the thatch-eves run:
To bend with apples the mossed cottage-trees,
And fill all fruit with ripeness to the core;
To swell the gourd, and plump the hazel shells
With a sweet kernel; to set budding more,
And still more, later flowers for the bees,
Until they think warm days will never cease,
For summer has o'er-brimmed their clammy cells.

Involve clients in planning and contributing to a service, led by a local clergyman. Perhaps the produce could be shared with a local charity.

Prepare a Harvest Supper.

Would the group enjoy a preserving food day, preparing fruit and vegetables for pickling?

Would the clients who enjoy craft activities, like to make bookmarks using pressed leaves?. Glue on leaves lightly and then cover with transparent plastic.

Organise an outing in a mini bus to view the autumn tints.

Remembrance Sunday

Remembrance Day originated on November 11th 1918, when the peace treaty was signed ending World War I
Many elderly people who lost relatives in both World Wars continue to receive comfort from ceremonies and services that honour their loved ones.

It will probably be important for the clients to watch the Remembrance services on the television. The group may like to share memories about wartime and perhaps sing some wartime songs.
You might like to read this famous poem to the group.

In Flanders' Fields

In Flanders' fields the poppies blow
Between the crosses, row on row,
That mark our place; and in the sky
The larks, still bravely singing, fly
Scarce heard amid the guns below.

We are the Dead. Short days ago
We lived, felt dawn, saw sunset glow,
Loved and were loved, and now we lie
In Flanders' Fields.

Take up our quarrel with the foe;
To you from failing hands we throw
The torch, be yours to hold it high.
If ye break faith with us who die
We shall not sleep, though poppies grow
In Flanders' fields.

John McCrae   1872-1918

Most of the Second World War songs are still in copyright so cannot be photocopied. The Winslow Press produce a set of large print song books which contain a section of war time favourites.
Once reminded of the first line clients will often be able to sing all the songs through to the end. Here are some suggestions:
'We'll meet again'
'You are my sunshine'
'The White cliffs of Dover'
'Roll out the barrel.'
'Bless them all.'

Chapter Seven Exercise and Relaxation

Rationale

Encouraging movement in elderly people is in most cases, of physical and mental benefit.

We aim to improve the condition of muscles and joints, and to help clients feel generally more alert and in trim.

Ideally, the advice of a physiotherapist will be sought in order to match exercises with the clients needs. By working with a group in this way, the services of a physiotherapist can benefit a large number of clients together.

Both exercise and relaxation sessions can also be pleasurable as a group activity.

Very anxious clients who learn relaxation techniques can feel more in control of their bodies, and they may then feel able to work towards overcoming problems such as panic attacks.

Armchair Exercises

Many benefits of exercise are obvious, but be aware of peoples limitations so that the exercises do not aggravate health problems.

Advise every one to stop when tired and have a physiotherapist to advise when possible.

The session will hopefully include lots of laughter and perhaps end with a sing song.

Time

Late morning is often a good time of day to choose when everyone is alert, waiting for lunch.

Preparation

Place chairs in a semicircle allowing as much room as possible for the movement of arms and legs. Have soft balls and bean bags available for part of the session. If possible, have someone to play the piano, or have a jolly music tape and a cassette player ready to switch on. Arrange for staff to join in if possible to confidence to clients. Make sure that anyone with hearing difficulties has their hearing aid in and switched on.

Switch on the music and Away we go!

Start with breathing exercises and slower movements
Suggested exercises to be repeated 3 or 4 times.
Follow bending in one direction by bending in the opposite direction
If in any doubt about the suitability of any exercise for any elderly client, ask the advice of the Doctor/Nurse/Physiotherapist.

Breathing in and out deeply and slowly.

Moving head from side to side slowly.

Looking up and down slowly.

Shrugging shoulders.

Hands on shoulders, circle elbows.

Wiggle fingers.

Shake hands.

Clap hands in rhythm.

Lift arm up and down, right and then left.

Wave up-stretched arms to the right and then to the left.

Lift knee up and down, right and then left.

Circle one foot and then the other.

Place feet flat on the ground and then lift up heels (up and down)

Bend over and try to touch toes.

Lift up both arms and reach back.

Finish the session playing football sitting down, or throwing the beanbag around the group.

For a change, try an exercise with a scarf.

Hold scarf at top corners and shake as if shaking a cloth.

Hold one corner and shake whilst lifting up and down.

Pretend the scarf is a duster.

Pretend to clean tables and shelves in one direction and then the other.

Pretend to clean windows in one direction and then the other.

Pretend to clean the ceiling.

Swap hands and start again.

Relaxation

Developing relaxation techniques is like any other skill, in that it needs practise. Those of us in our fifties or younger are likely to have had some practise: during antenatal classes or perhaps at a yoga evening class.
The elderly clients now attending day centres or living in nursing homes may not have had the experience of learning relaxation techniques before, but if they take part in the sessions on a regular basis, the skill can develop.
The Community Psychiatric Nurse can advise.

Whilst lying on the floor on cushions may be the ideal position for the client, relaxing in a comfortable armchair is a good alternative.

Commercial relaxation tapes are excellent and can be bought in many chemists, bookshops and healthfood shops. They can be played to the group and do not then need a leader, just someone on hand should anyone need help. These tapes are especially suitable for well established groups.

To lead a Relaxation group you will need to at least have attended relaxation sessions and learnt the skill yourself.
Prepare well by making the setting as pleasant as possible and choosing a suitable piece of music. My favourite is a recording of familiar classical harp music.

During the session you could develop a scenario with the group. Take about 20 minutes.

Ask the group to relax back in their chairs and close their eyes, and begin the scenario,

For Example

Imagine you are back at a peaceful place from the past:
Walking through the woods on a spring day,
Sitting in a deckchair by the seaside, or
Rocking in a rocking chair at your grandmothers.

- Let your body go limp.

- Breath deeply in and out.

- In through your nose and out through your mouth.

- In and out, in and out, in and out.

- Start at your toes and first tighten and then relax each part of your body in turn.

- Feel the tension flow from your feet and legs.

- Squeeze your buttocks and relax.

- Pull in your stomach muscles and relax.

- Relax as you breath out.

- There is often a great deal of tension around the shoulders.
  Feel them relaxing down.

- Breathing in and out slowly, allowing tension to flow away. (Repeat)

- Clench your hands and relax your hands and fingers.

- Screw up your face and relax.

- Listen to the music and relax.

- Breath in and out, allowing the tension to flow away as you breath out

Slowly Bring Everybody Back

- First wiggle your toes, gradually move each part of your body in turn.

In your own time move, and when you are ready, open your eyes.

Hopefully, most people will have enjoyed the session, but like everything else that we do with our clients not everyone will want to join in.
It is important with these sessions, that they take place in a neutral space and are free from interruptions.
Eventually the clients may find relaxing easy at different times of the day and night.

Chapter Eight Miscellaneous

The final section of this book contains some pages which can be photocopied for use when setting up an activities programme. (i.e. pages 102, 105, 107)

The Client Social Sheet can be filled in by the appropriate member of staff and made available to the activities organiser (with client permission). The development of the clients participation in social activities can be recorded in the overall care plan.

The Activities Timetable and Poster can be used to plan and publicise the events.

New beginnings and Achievements for over Sixties

We are fascinated with the achievements of children and expect bright young people to continue to blossom. This does not always happen. Sometimes young people destined for greatness showed no promise in their early years and sometimes people in their 60's 70's and 80's find the motivation to develop an interest and become an expert in their field.

In reality, no real age barriers exist. Older people have physical problems as do younger people, but apart from having lived longer and so have more experience, being older does not mean that one feels any different or that one cannot learn new skills.

People from all ages seem to enjoy discussing the achievements of the personalities on this list. I have collected this information from newspapers and books over the last few years, and believe it to be correct.

Age	
60	Emmeline Pankhurst won votes for women.
61	Sheila Bick from Gloucestershire made a career move and trained to be a reflexologist.
62	Louis Pasteur first injected against Rabies
63	Rosanna Corta from Viterbo in Italy gave birth to a son.
64	Henrik Ibsen, great Norwegian playwright wrote the brilliant play 'The Master Builder'
65	Sir Francis Chichester made the first solo sailing trip around the world
66	Dancer, Josephine Baker, returned from Paris to America and gave a sensational performance, in a body stocking.
67	Tolstoy had his first bicycle lesson.
68	Queen Victoria started learning Hindustani.
69	Ronald Reagan became 40th President of the U.S.A.
70	Copernicus published first and last book, The analysis of Planetary Movement.
71	Michelangelo appointed chief architect of Saint Peters in Rome.
72	Gandhi launched 'Quit India Movement' that led to India's independence in 1947
73	Claude Monet started his famous set of water lily paintings.
74	Elizabeth Arden was still doing head stands daily as part of her yoga exercises.

75	Agatha Cristie wrote her autobiography.
76	Marc Chagall, famous Russian born artist, started work on the magnificent painting adorning the Opera House ceiling in Paris.
77	Doris Morse, from Penarth in South Wales started a new job on the fish counter, at a local supermarket..
78	Ayatollah Khomeini came to power
79	Christopher Wren finished Saint Pauls.
80	Grandma Moses had her first art exhibition.
81	Jack Warner appeared as Dixon of Dock Green on television.
82	William Gladstone was elected Prime Minister.
83	Charlie Chapman won an Oscar.
84	Coco Chanel, fashion designer, was head of her company.
85	Mae West starred in a film called 'Sextette'.
86	Joe Ashmore from New Zealand made his first Bungee Jump.
87	Dame Edith Evans performed in the musical 'The Slipper and the Rose'.
88	George Lush in Hatfield, Herts. obtained Grade D in A level G.C.E.Italian
89	Bertrand Russell was imprisoned for demonstrating against the Hydrogen Bomb.
90	Gerty Edwards Land passed her driving test in Colne Lancs.
91	Helena Rubinstein started writing her memoirs 'my Life For Beauty'.
92	Michel Engere Cheveul published works on the Theories of Matter
93	George Bernard Shaw wrote his play 'Far Fetched Fables'.
94	Bertrand Russell resigned from the Labour Party as a protest at its support for the Vietnam War.
95	Hilda Franks first exhibited paintings, at St. Martins Church, Croydon.
97	Fred Streeter was broadcasting a weekly gardening programme. programme on the radio.
98	Dimitrion Yordanidis from Greece ran and finished a marathon in Athens.
99	Hildegarde Ferra from the U.S.A. parachuted at Mokuleia.
100	Winifred Clark on the eve of her 100th birthday, married Albert Smith aged 80.
101	Harry Bidwell from Brighton divorced his wife aged 65.
102	Minnie Munro married Dudley Reid age 83 in N.S.W, Australia.
105	Edward Newson from Hove, East Sussex, retired from his property management business, but continued to drive his car.
110	Charlotte Hughes from Redcor, Yorkshire flew in Concorde as a birthday present.
114	Jeanne Louise Calmont portrayed herself in a 1990 film about a girl who met Van Gough (a true experience from Madame Calmonts life)

Client Social Care Sheet

NAME   CENTRE/HOME   D.O.B

What name would you like to be known by ?

What hobbies or social activities have you enjoyed in the past?

TICK LIST

Home Care	Going to the Pub.
Cooking	Music / Concerts
Gardening	Reading
Flowercrafts	Arts / Crafts
Needlework	Day Trips / Holidays
Knitting	Church Activities
Pets	

What are your favourite T.V. / Radio programmes?

What is your favourite type of music?

Previous Career / Employment.

What new hobbies would you like to try?

Special Considerations.

Sample - for care plan

Client Social Care Sheet

NAME Miss Theresa Walsh   CENTRE/HOME The Willows   D.O.B 6/2/29

What name would you like to be known by? Theresa

What hobbies or social activities have you enjoyed in the past?

TICK LIST

Home Care	Going to the Pub.
Cooking	Music / Concerts ✓
Gardening	Reading ✓
Flowercrafts ✓	Arts / Crafts
Needlework ✓	Day Trips / Holidays
Knitting	Church Activities ✓
Pets	

What are your favourite T.V. / Radio programmes?

Quizzes like 'Countdown'

What is your favourite type of music?

Classical

Previous Career / Employment.

Headmistress at a girls school in Ireland.

What new hobbies would you like to try?

Painting.

Special Considerations.

Diabetic
History of falls
Feels uncomfortable in mixed company

Activities Timetable

Day	Morning	Afternoon	Evening
Monday			
Tuesday			
Wednesday			
Thursday			
Friday			
Saturday			
Sunday			

Sample

Activities Timetable The Willows

Day	Morning	Afternoon	Evening
Monday	Armchair Exercises Main Lounge 11am	Pottery Craft Room 3pm	
Tuesday	Holy Communion Small Lounge 11am	Mini-bus to Lydney 2pm	
Wednesday	Indoor Bowls Main Lounge 11am	Residents Meeting Dining Room 3pm	
Thursday	Library Van 10:30am	Painting Group Craft Room 3pm	Slide Show (Weston Trip) Dining Room 6pm
Friday	Armchair Exercises Main lounge 11am	Knit and Natter Small Lounge 3pm	
Saturday	Coffee Morning Dining Room 10am		
Sunday			Choir to Entertain Dining Room 6pm

Please Join Us !

You may reproduce this page

Sample

Please Join Us !

Residents Meeting
Today 3 p.m.
in
The Lounge

A Newsletter for the Home or Centre

This can be a regular group effort, involving staff, clients and their families, encouraging communication and developing skills. A quarterly edition is probably best at first, rather than publishing weekly or monthly.

A group can meet regularly to discuss progress and distribute the jobs to be done, including: collecting articles, recipes, forthcoming events, funny incidents, illustrations etc. Someone must type the contributions, layout the copy and duplicate the final result. The group may decide to ask a local business to advertise to help with costs.

The Willows Newsletter

sample

Summer 1997   no.2

Dear All,

Thank you for the interest shown in the Willows Newsletter, which we hope to produce bi-monthly next year. We would welcome any suggestions or contributions for the autumn edition, to be handed in to Joan by 6th September. Editor

News and Views

WE HAVE RAISED THE MONEY FOR THE MINI BUS!!

At the next residents meeting, to be held on July 6th at 3pm. in the dining room, we will hear from Matron when the new mini bus will arrive and discuss its usage. Please bring your ideas for outings along to the meeting.

The Friends of The Willows are hoping to reform soon so would like to hear from anyone who is interested in becoming involved. A meeting will be arranged soon. Watch the notice board for details

The new timetable of leisure activities will be on the board by the 5th June.

Comings and Goings

Welcome to Gillian Brown who is to be the new night nurse on Thursday and Saturday night. Gillian, who used to work at the General hospital before she had her baby, has lived in the village for 10 years.

We will miss care assistant, John Jones when he leaves at the end of the month, but wish him luck in his new career with Marks and Spencer.

THE COFFEE LOUNGE

*Home made cakes,
freshly ground coffee
Lunches and teas
Take away meals & catering*

Gallery Needlework

**For all your tapestry
& embroidery requirements
also Picture Framing and
daylight magnifying lamps**

Crossword

Answers over page

ACROSS
1 Mate
5 Beach particles
8 Concise, of few words
9 Herb
11 Staple Indian food
13 Situation
15 Sporting trophy
16 Sheltered harbour
17 Household animal
18 Give money to
19 Portion of cake
21 Savour
23 Dispel (fears)
26 Singing voice
28 Splendid
29 Lacking flavour
30 Blood
31 ____ Edmonds, TV star

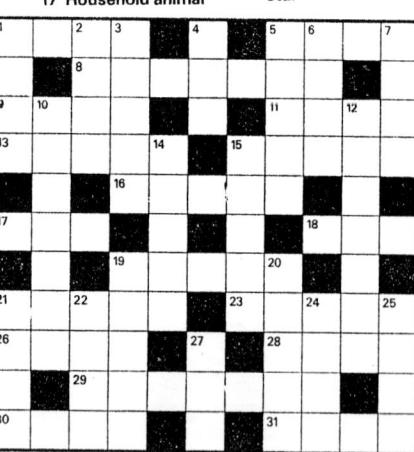

DOWN
1 Group of tents
2 Forearm bone
3 Game, contest
4 Sink a snooker ball
5 Alarm signal
6 Corrosive liquid
7 Fight between two
10 Unlawful
12 Mobile home
14 'Golden' bird of prey
15 Islamic pilgrimage city
19 Fourteen pounds
20 Pixie-like
21 Strong flavour
22 Arouse
24 Outdoor swimming-pool
25 Shriek
27 Coalmine

Useful Contacts

Age Exchange 11 Blackheath Village London S.E.3 Tel 0181 3183504 - Reminiscience training and equipment.

Age Concern England Astral House, 1268 London Rd. London SW16 4EJ Tel. 0181 679 8000

Alzheimer's Disease Soc. 2nd Floor, Gordon House, 10 Greencoat Place London SW1P 1PH Tel. 0171 306 0606

The Stroke Ass. CHSA House, Whitecross St. London EC1V 3QP Tel. 0171 490 7999

Council and Care for the Elderly, Twyman House, 16 Bonny St. London NW1 9PG Tel 0171 485 1550

Council for Music in Hospitals, 74 Queens Rd Hersham Surrey KT12 5LW Tel 01424 442500 - arranges musical events in hospitals, Homes and Centres.

Extend, 22 Maltings Drive, Wheathampstead, Herts.AL4 8QJ Tel 01582 832760 - promotes exercise to music for elderly people.

Fred Aldous Ltd, 37, Lever St. Manchester M60 1UX tel 00161 2362477- craft supplier.

Help the Aged St James Walk, Clerkenwell Green, London EC1R OBE Tel 0171 253 0253.

Parkinson's Disease Soc. 36 Portland Place, London W1N 3DG Tel 0171 383 3513.

Royal National Institute for the Blind, 224, Great Portland St. London W1N 6AA Tel 0171 388 1266.

Royal National Institute for the Deaf , 19/23 Featherstone St. London ECLY 8SL Tel 0171 2968000.

British Chess Federation, 9a Grand Parade, St Leonards on Sea, East Sussex TN38 Tel 01424 442500.

Nottingham Rehab., Ludlow Hill Road, West Bridford, Nottingham NG2 6HD Tel 01602 452345. A wide range of craft materials and equipment.

T.F.H. 76 Barracks Rd. Sandy Lane Ind. Est. Stourport on Severn Worcs. DY13 3QB Tel 01299 827820 - Resource Equipment, in particular, Multi Sensory Enviroment.

Winslow Telford Rd, Bicester, Oxon OX6 OTS Tel)1869 244644 Wide range of equipment relevant to providing leisure activities for elderly people.

Winsor and Newton, Whitefriars Avenue, Wealdstone, Harrow HA8 7 HF Tel 0181 4274343 - Art Materials.

Bibliography

Bender M, Norris A &Bauckham P, *Groupwork with the Elderly principals and Practice*, Winslow Press, Bicester, 1987.

Briscoe T, *Develop an Activities Programme*, Winslow Press, Bicester 1991.

Clarke A & Hollands J, *Leisure Later Life and Homes*, Counsel and Care London NW1 9PG 1995.

Comfort A, *A Good Age*, Mitchel Beazley 1977.

Counsel and Care, *Not Only Bingo*, Report 1993.

Davidson F, *Alzheimer's, A practical guide for carers, to help you through the day*, Judy Piaticus Publishers Ltd. London.

Denham M, *Care of the Long Stay Elderly Patient*, Chapman and Hall 1991.

Enright D & Rawlinson, *The Oxford Book of Friendship*, Oxford University Press 1991.

Help the Aged, *Giving good Care*
(excellent Booklet for care assistants which includes some ideas for promoting leisure interests).

Hong C S, *Activities Digest*, Winslow Press, Bicester, 1989.

Liebman M, *Art Therapy for Groups*, Routledge 1989.

McCourt V, *Cherish the Memory*, Nursing Times Article 20/7/94.

Murphy A, *Woking with Elderly People*, Souvenir Press 1994.

Norris A, *Reminiscence with Elderly People*, Winslow Press 1986.

Oxford University Press, *Dictionary of Quotations* 1941

Ruskin College, *It's Never too Late*, 1993.
(learning Pack available from Agewell, Ruskin College, Oxford Oxl 2HE)

Sherman M, *The Reminiscence Quiz Book*, Winslow Press, Bicester, 1991.

Walsh D, *Groupwork Activities*, Winslow Press, Bicester, 1993

Windmill V, *Caring for the Elderly*, Longman 1992.

A

Activities Programme - Content · 18
Activities Timetable · 104
Armchair Exercises · 96

B

Beads: Clay · 47; Papier-mâché · 46
Behaviour: Disruptive · 17
Bibliography · 110
Bingo · 84
BlockPrinting · 57
Body Language · 16; Awareness of · 16
Book of Memories · 28
Bouquet Garni Sachets · 80

C

Cardiovascular Diseases · 10
Christmas Activities · 89
Christmas Projects · 86; Christmas decoration · 87; Christmas pomander · 87; Fabric tree decorations · 88; Golden angels · 88; Wrapping Presents · 86
Clay · 12
Client Social Care Sheet · 102, 103
Communication Problems · 11
Concert: Organise · 83
Consultation: Client · 18
Cooking · 79
Crepe Paper Roses · 70
Crochet · 77
Cross Stitch · 76

D

Day Trips · 82
Deafness · 12
Decorating Paper: Decorated Paper · 60; Marbling · 54; Monoprinting · 55; Stencilling · 58
Decoupage · 64; 3-D Modern decoupage · 65
Dementia · 13
Depression · 12
Diabetes Mellitus · 10
Discussion Groups · 12, 16, 23; Current affairs · 23
Disruptive Behaviour · 17
Dough Craft · 53

E

Easter Projects · 91; Egg decorating · 92
Egg Decorating · 92
Events and Entertainment · 83

Exercise: Armchair · 13
Exercise With a Scarf · 97

F

Flower Arranging · 68
Flowers: Preserving · 66
Friendship · 9
Funding · 18

G

Games: Flipchart · 20; Guess the shopping bag · 21; Memory · 23; Royal quiz · 21; table · 20; Word · 20
Gardening · 80
Gift Bags · 60
Greeting Card · 62
Group Activity: Setting up of · 15
Group Meetings · 8

H

Harvest Festival · 93
Health · 10
Health and Safety · 78
Health and Welfare · 24
Horoscopes · 23

J

Jewellery Making · 46

K

Knitting · 71

L

Leaf Prints · 56
leisure Time: improving the quality of · 7
Loner: Catering for · 9
Lung Disease · 10

M

Manicure · 8
Marbling · 54
Mental Exercise: Rationale · 19
Monoprinting · 55
Motivation: Lack of · 17

Multi-Sensory Environments · 14
Muscle Power: Decline in · 10
Musical Quiz · 12

N

New Beginnings · 100
Newsletter · 108

O

Osteoarthritis · 10
Outings · 82

P

Painting: Points to remember · 51; Therapeutic · 52; Water colour · 50
Painting Sessions: Therapeutic · 13
Paper Flowers · 70
Papier-mâché · 63
Parkinson's Disease · 11
Patchwork · 74
Pets · 8
Photograph Gallery · 84
Poetry · 42
Poster · 106
Pot Pourri · 12
Potpourri · 69
Pottery · 48
Preserving Flowers · 66
Pressed Flowers · 67; Decorate a small box · 67
Pressure Sores · 11

Q

Quilt · 74
Quiz: Christmas · 89; Christmas music · 89; Christmas sound · 89; Reminiscence · 26

R

Reality Orientation Board · 13
Relaxation · 98

Reluctant Group Members · 17
Remembrance Sunday · 94
Reminiscence · 13, 25; Benefits to Nursing and Care Staff · 25; Cue questions · 26; Equipment · 25; Quiz · 26; Suggested Topics · 26
Royal Family, The · 23
Rug · 72; Latch hooked · 73; Traditional rag · 72

S

Sawdust Kiln From a Biscuit Tin · 47
Sensory Problems · 12
Sight Impairment · 12
Singing · 38
Slide Show · 83
Snoezelen · 14
Speaker · 83
Sports Day · 83
Stencilled Stationery · 59
Stroke · 11

T

Table Centre · 68
Teapot Card · 62
Thumb Pot · 48

U

Useful Contacts · 109

V

Video Club · 83

W

Welfare Rights · 24